Cambridge Elements ≡

Elements in Historical Theory and Practice
edited by
Daniel Woolf
Queen's University, Ontario

WRITING THE HISTORY OF THE AFRICAN DIASPORA

Toyin Falola
The University of Texas at Austin

CAMBRIDGE
UNIVERSITY PRESS

Shaftesbury Road, Cambridge CB2 8EA, United Kingdom

One Liberty Plaza, 20th Floor, New York, NY 10006, USA

477 Williamstown Road, Port Melbourne, VIC 3207, Australia

314–321, 3rd Floor, Plot 3, Splendor Forum, Jasola District Centre,
New Delhi – 110025, India

103 Penang Road, #05–06/07, Visioncrest Commercial, Singapore 238467

Cambridge University Press is part of Cambridge University Press & Assessment,
a department of the University of Cambridge.

We share the University's mission to contribute to society through the pursuit of
education, learning and research at the highest international levels of excellence.

www.cambridge.org
Information on this title: www.cambridge.org/9781009475686
DOI: 10.1017/9781009442084

© Toyin Falola 2024

When citing this work, please include a reference to the DOI 10.1017/9781009442084

First published 2024

A catalogue record for this publication is available from the British Library.

ISBN 978-1-009-47568-6 Hardback
ISBN 978-1-009-44211-4 Paperback
ISSN 2634-8616 (online)
ISSN 2634-8608 (print)

Writing the History of the African Diaspora

Elements in Historical Theory and Practice

DOI: 10.1017/9781009442084
First published online: May 2024

Toyin Falola
The University of Texas at Austin

Author for correspondence: Toyin Falola, toyinfalola@austin.utexas.edu

Abstract: This Element is an analysis of the African Diaspora. It will define the African Diaspora and how the concepts behind the term came to be socially and historically engineered. The African diaspora is then placed into a broader historical context where the diverse, global, and overlapping histories of Africa's ancient-ongoing diasporas will be explored. In particular, themes of injustice, agency, resistance, and diversity (regarding people, diasporas, and experiences) will feature heavily. Through this exploration, this Element will interrogate dominating narratives regarding African diaspora-related discourse, seeking to address prevailing ideas that inadequately capture the true complexity and nuance of the subject. It does so to construct a more comprehensive understanding of the subject matter while lining out a more holistic approach to thinking about the very nature of "diaspora." Finally, this Element will analyze the present circumstances of the African diaspora, bringing into conversation a progressively global and connected world.

Keywords: History and theory, research methods and approaches, history of ideas, global history

ISBNs: 9781009475686 (HB), 9781009442114 (PB), 9781009442084 (OC)
ISSNs: 2634-8616 (online), 2634-8608 (print)

Contents

Introduction

The history of the African Diaspora, while extensively studied, remains multifaceted, with much to discover. It is crucial to understand how this history has been constructed, with many scholars utilizing a Eurocentric framework, thus, sidelining significant aspects like the history of free people of African descent and their contributions.

Two major perspectives dominate the discourse. The first emphasizes the agency of Africans, viewing migrations as driven by desires for economic opportunity and personal freedom. The second underscores the brutalities of the transatlantic slave trade, presenting it as the foundational event that shaped the experiences of Africans and their descendants. By embracing diverse perspectives, we can gain a more complete understanding of the African Diaspora and its significance.[1]

The term "African Diaspora" often gets constrained to its geographical connotations, sidelining its cultural and historical depth. Beyond mere geography, the African Diaspora connects individuals through shared experiences and cultural ties. The identity formation of those within the diaspora is dynamic, and ever-evolving with global and historical shifts.

Despite significant contributions to adopted cultures worldwide, ranging from arts to politics, the African Diaspora still grapples with challenges such as restrictive immigration policies and gentrification. Recognizing the agency and resilience of the diaspora population allows for a richer global cultural and historical understanding.[2]

The viewpoints on the transatlantic slave trade and precolonial migration in Africa offer divergent historical, cultural, and social narratives. The transatlantic slave trade, a somber and distressing period in history, encompassed the coerced and merciless transportation of millions of Africans to the Americas, Europe and the Caribbean. This involuntary movement was marked by intense aggression, dehumanization, and the erasure of individual and cultural identities, resulting in a lasting impact of trauma, grief, and ongoing racial and socioeconomic inequalities. The slave trade had a substantial impact on African societies, resulting in substantial population loss and enduring economic and political destabilization. It has emerged as a key topic in conversations surrounding race, colonialism, and reparations, deeply embedded in the shared recollections of African diaspora communities.

Notably, precolonial migrations within Africa were primarily voluntary, motivated by various factors, including trade, exploration, territorial expansion, or

---

[1] Chidozie Chukwuokolo, "Afrocentrism or Eurocentrism: The dilemma of African development," *OGIRISI: A New Journal of African Studies* 6 (2009): 24–39.

[2] Cameron J. Monroe, "Power and agency in precolonial African states," *Annual Review of Anthropology* 42 (2013): 17–35.

environmental challenges. These migrations resulted from the inherent dynamics of African societies, fostering cultural diversity and facilitating exchange throughout the continent. They played a crucial role in disseminating languages, customs, technologies, and knowledge, greatly enhancing established communities and giving rise to new ones. In contrast to the transatlantic slave trade, these movements demonstrate the capacity of African societies to adapt and engage with their surroundings and other cultures. The migrations have left a lasting impact on African cultures and histories, showcasing their richness and diversity. However, it is important to acknowledge that these migrations also brought complexities and challenges.

The contrasting viewpoints on these two historical phenomena can be attributed to their significant impacts and enduring legacies. Although precolonial migrations are often praised for their positive impact on the cultural diversity of Africa, the transatlantic slave trade is widely recognized for the profound and tragic consequences it had on the continent and its inhabitants. From a scholarly perspective, the focus on the transatlantic slave trade has often overshadowed the accounts of precolonial Africa, resulting in a distorted understanding of African history that primarily emphasizes victimization and colonization. On the other hand, precolonial migrations highlight African history's vibrant and ever-changing aspects, revealing a continent filled with a wide range of actions and variations. Grasping these contrasting narratives is essential for a well-rounded understanding of Africa's history, one that recognizes the people's significant obstacles and their indomitable spirit.

The modern era witnesses an "emerging global African Diaspora" characterized by diversity, mobility, and interconnectedness. This new wave of migration brings both opportunities and challenges but holds the promise of reshaping global culture and understanding.

The African Diaspora narrative undoubtedly represents an intricate story of worldwide migration and cultural development, firmly grounded in the historical movement of individuals from Africa. Of all the experiences, one that stands out is that of Black Africans from West Africa, which carries immense historical, cultural, and sociopolitical significance. This region played a pivotal role in the transatlantic slave trade. This significant event profoundly influenced the course of history for millions of people and left a lasting imprint on the world, thereby justifying the emphasis on Black Africans from West Africa in this Element. It is also ideal because it enables a thorough examination of a diaspora segment that has played a crucial role in shaping modern societies, particularly in the Americas and Europe. The rich heritage of West African communities, carried through the harrowing experiences of slavery, has deeply influenced diverse facets of culture, economy, and social structures in their adopted countries, thus, rendering their narrative an indispensable element of the broader tapestry of human history and cultural interchange.

By focusing on this particular group, this Element can potentially deepen our comprehension of the African diaspora in multiple ways. Firstly, it offers a perspective to critically analyze the enduring impacts of the slave trade. The profound effects of the transatlantic slave trade on both the African continent and the diaspora cannot be overstated. By directing our attention to communities originating from West Africa, we can delve into a comprehensive examination of these far-reaching outcomes. This encompasses the historical backdrop and the lasting cultural connections and changes that connect these diaspora communities to their West African roots. For example, the preservation and evolution of West African cultural practices in diasporic communities have created diverse and dynamic cultures that showcase the strength and flexibility of these communities. Thus, centering on this particular group enables a more intricate comprehension of diasporic experiences, steering clear of the oversimplifications that can arise when studying a varied continent such as Africa. It also provides an opportunity to explore current challenges these communities face, including racial identity and social integration issues. Understanding their current situation in a global context is essential.

1 What is the History of the African Diaspora?

Introduction: Defining and Understanding the African Diaspora

A relatively simplistic definition of the African Diaspora is an international community of individuals of African descent whose geographic dispersion emerged as a result of the transatlantic slave trade and other ensuing periods of involuntary and voluntary migration. This dispersal commenced around the sixteenth century and continues up till recent times. This definition satisfies the curiosity of an average inquiry, but it does not do justice to what or who should be included in the term "African Diaspora." The simple definition subsumes a lot of information. It is important to recognize that identifying members of the African Diaspora requires an understanding of the forced migration of millions of Africans from various parts of their continent to the Americas, the Caribbean, and other parts of the world, and it includes the voluntary migration of African people in search of better economic and social opportunities.[3] Through the Indian Ocean, Africans also moved to Asia and Australia.

To understand the African Diaspora, it is important to begin with the history of the transatlantic slave trade and how it affected Africa and the

---

[3] Colin Palmer, "The African Diaspora," *The Black Scholar* 30, 3–4 (2000): 56–59.

Americas.[4] The slave trade involved millions of people forcibly removed from Africa, their endurance of the harsh conditions of the Middle Passage, and the adaptations of enslaved Africans who were forced to accommodate new cultures and ways of life in their new homes. The African Diaspora also affected the cultures, societies, and economies of places where people of African descent ultimately settled. People of African descent made unique contributions to the development of local music, art, literature, and other cultural forms.[5] An understanding of the African Diaspora also involves the ways in which people of African descent have been treated and discriminated against around the world.

"Unfinished Migrations: Reflections on the African diaspora and the Making of the Modern World"[6] provides a valuable starting point for understanding the complexities of the African Diaspora. In their article, Patterson and Kelley highlight the need for a diasporic identity that connects people to a common geography, which challenges traditional notions of the African Diaspora and encourages a more nuanced understanding of the dispersal of African people throughout the world. They argue that dispersal does not necessarily lead to a diaspora. For a diaspora to exist, there must be a diasporic identity linking the diaspora's constituent parts with a common homeland. Contrary to some suggestions, the notion of an African Diaspora that recognized Africa as its homeland was not always a natural development, rather, it had to be socially and historically created.

The concept of an African Diaspora is a complex and dynamic interplay of political, social, and cultural factors – and the forced migration of millions of Africans across the Atlantic during the transatlantic slave trade was a key factor in shaping that diaspora. Slavery's legacy, along with the persistent discrimination and marginalization faced by people of African descent in the Americas and elsewhere, were also important factors in shaping the development of the African Diaspora. The idea of an African Diaspora was further defined by the efforts of Black intellectuals, activists, and political leaders who sought to reclaim their African heritage and assert their place in the world as a people with a shared history and cultural identity.[7] Their work helped to create a shared sense of belonging and identity among people of African descent, establishing Africa as a symbol of hope, pride, and belonging for people of African descent around the world.

---

[4] Toyin Falola, *The African Diaspora: Slavery, Modernity, and Globalization* (Rochester: University of Rochester Press, 2013).

[5] Theresa A. Singleton, "African Diaspora in archaeology," in Tejumola Olaniyan and James Sweet, (eds.), *The African Diaspora and the Disciplines* (Bloomington: Indiana University Press, 2010), 119–141.

[6] Tiffany Ruby Patterson and Robin D. G. Kelley, "Unfinished migrations: Reflections on the African Diaspora and the making of the modern world," *African Studies Review* 43, 1 (2000): 11–45.

[7] Charles Pete Banner-Haley, *From Du Bois to Obama: African American Intellectuals in the Public Forum* (Carbondale: Southern Illinois University Press, 2010).

Despite the important role that social and cultural forces played in shaping the notion of an African Diaspora, the idea still revolves around a deliberate and conscious effort to create a shared sense of identity and community among people of African descent. This is why it is important to evaluate the history of the African Diaspora, drawing from different perspectives and ideas, and to evaluate the results for a more robust and complete understanding.

Perspectives on Precolonial Migrations and Understanding the Transatlantic Slave Trade

Precolonial migrations in the fifteenth century were characterized by the movement of people across the Atlantic and the establishment of trade networks connecting the Americas, Europe, and Africa.[8] The transatlantic slave trade was a major part of this process, and millions were forcibly removed from Africa to work as slaves in the Americas. This trade had a lasting impact on the history and culture of the African Diaspora, not only in the Americas but also in Africa. The transatlantic slave trade affected Africa in many ways, introducing economic and demographic disruptions as well as social and cultural transformations caused by a massive forced migration. The study of precolonial migrations has been an important area of research for historians, anthropologists, and other scholars because understanding precolonial migrations and the transatlantic slave trade is essential for understanding the history and culture of the African Diaspora. It is also relevant for understanding the ongoing legacy of colonization, capitalism, and empire.[9]

Philip Curtin and Olivette Otele have made significant contributions to the study of precolonial migrations. Curtin focused on the larger context of developing world systems, and Otele explored transatlantic slavery's impact on contemporary questions of migration. Other bodies of research have critically examined precolonial migrations and the transatlantic slave trade, and they have even shown how the parts of Africa that were most affected by the slave trade had more pronounced precolonial characteristics, such as the initial composition of their ethnic groups.

Curtin's work, *The Atlantic Slave Trade: A Census*,[10] serves as a comprehensive study of the transatlantic slave trade between the sixteenth and the nineteenth centuries. Curtin's book presents a detailed analysis based on extensive research and examinations of primary sources, such as shipping records and other historical

---

[8] Kenneth Swindell, "People on the move in West Africa: From pre-colonial polities to post-independence states," in Robert Cohen, (ed.), *The Cambridge Survey of World Migration* (Cambridge: University of Cambridge, 1995), 196–202.

[9] Falola, *The African Diaspora*.

[10] Philip D. Curtin, *The Atlantic Slave Trade: A Census* (Madison: University of Wisconsin Press, 1972).

documents. Curtin presents the slave trade as a complex process shaped by economic, political, and social factors. He emphasizes that trade was not a passive process, contrary to different historical positions; it was actively driven by the demand for labor in the Americas and the supply of enslaved people from Africa, and African rulers and traders were actively involved in the process.

Curtin has leveraged statistical and historical input to identify the economic forces driving the transatlantic slave trade. He finds that the demand for labor in the Americas was driven by the growth of plantation systems, which required large numbers of workers to cultivate crops such as sugar, tobacco, and cotton. Without enough labor to work in the Americas, Africa became a source of forceful recruitment. The supply of enslaved labor increased due to demand and economic incentives.

African rulers and traders saw the slave trade as a means of acquiring wealth and power, and they supplied enslaved people to European traders in exchange for guns, textiles, alcohol, and other goods. Some African societies engaged in the slave trade to acquire captive soldiers, domestic servants, or subjects for human sacrifice. Curtin argues that the slave trade was not a passive process and that economic and political factors actively drove it. European traders were only part of the equation – African rulers and traders also played a significant role. Curtin's perspective on precolonial migration and the transatlantic slave trade departs from traditional narratives that described a trade driven solely by European activity.

Curtin also considers the social and demographic consequences of the transatlantic slave trade. He argues that the slave trade had a significant impact on the demographic structure of African societies. Family and community structures were disrupted as enslaved people were taken from their homes, which affected the social fabric of the societies by leaving behind large numbers of orphans and widows. The slave trade also disrupted traditional patterns of marriage, fertility, and inheritance, leaving a lasting impact on the demographic structure of African societies. The exchange of goods and weapons also had an impact on the economic structure of African societies, which altered the balance of power among different groups, creating new economic and social hierarchies.

The Atlantic Slave Trade is widely viewed as a seminal work in the field of African and Atlantic history, but it has some shortcomings. Curtin's book focuses on statistics and data from the slave trade, identifying the number of enslaved people transported, the origins and destinations of shipments, and the mortality rates of enslaved people during transport.[11] These facts are important for understanding the scope and scale of the trade, but some scholars argue that they overlook the human experiences of those who were enslaved. Curtin's

---

[11] Curtin, *The Atlantic Slave Trade*.

book fails to explore the psychological and emotional trauma experienced by enslaved people who were taken from their homes and families, forced to live in inhumane conditions during transport, and exploited on the plantations. He largely overlooks enslavement's impact on a sense of identity and community or how the enslaved coped with their trauma.

Curtin's perspective largely focused on the activities of European traders and economic factors that drove the slave trade, giving little attention to the perspectives and experiences of African societies. His book does not provide an in-depth exploration of the motives behind African societies that participated in the slave trade or the trade's impact on African societies. It also ignores how the cultural and political diversity of African societies shaped their participation in the slave trade.

Some scholars have criticized Curtin for failing to provide a nuanced understanding of African societies and their role in the slave trade. These critics[12] argue that his work portrays African societies as passive and homogenous, which ignores the diversity of cultures and political systems that existed in Africa at the time of the slave trade. Curtin's work does not give enough attention to the complexity and diversity of African societies or the ways in which these societies participated in the slave trade. Its analysis ignores how different African cultures and political systems shaped the trade.

Olivette Otele is another author who offers constructive perspectives on African migration and the transatlantic slave trade. Otele's *African Europeans: An Untold History*[13] explores a part of history that few people know about or believe in. The book highlights the contributions and experiences of African Europeans over the centuries, challenging long-held assumptions about European history. Otele is one of the few scholars who studies the history of Black people in Europe. Her important book adds to a small but noteworthy group of publications that discuss Black history in Europe. *African Europeans* begins with a discussion of African enslavement and how Africans were viewed differently, as less valuable than other humans. This remains an issue in the present day, driving the Black Lives Matter movement to engage in protests because Black lives are still not treated as equal.[14] Otele's book explains how race was invented and applied to control and devalue Black lives, allowing them to be killed without consequence.

---

[12] See, for instance, David Henige, "Measuring the immeasurable: The atlantic slave trade, West African population and the Pyrrhonian critic," *Journal of African History* 27, 2 (1986): 295–313; Paul E. Lovejoy, "The volume of the atlantic slave trade: A synthesis," *Journal of African History* 23, 4 (1982): 473–502; Joseph E. Inikori, "Measuring the atlantic slave trade: An assessment of Curtin and Anstey," *Journal of African History* 17, 2 (1976): 197–223.

[13] Olivette Otele, *African Europeans: An Untold History* (New York: Basic Books, 2021).

[14] Lanier Frush Holt and Matthew D. Sweitzer, "More than a Black and White issue: Ethnic identity, social dominance orientation, and support for the Black Lives Matter movement," *Self and Identity* 19, 1 (2020): 16–31.

A key strength of Otele's work is her use of diverse, interdisciplinary sources that include literature, art, and archaeology, bringing the experiences and contributions of African Europeans to light. This broad-ranging approach offers a nuanced, multifaceted view of the subject that is often missing from traditional historical accounts. Another important aspect of *African Europeans* is Otele's emphasis on the agency of African Europeans and their ability to shape their own experiences, influencing their communities and broader societies.[15] This perspective challenges traditional views of African Europeans as passive victims of colonialism and the transatlantic slave trade, highlighting the resilience, strength, and creativity of their communities. The book's chronological scope is also noteworthy, covering the period from ancient times to the present day. Readers can gain a deep understanding of the historical context and the evolving experiences of African Europeans over time.

Although Otele's *African Europeans* is a thought-provoking and well-written book, it is primarily focused on Western Europe. It makes a significant contribution to our understanding of Western European history, but it pays limited attention to other parts of the continent. This leaves readers looking for additional information about the experiences of African Europeans in Eastern Europe and elsewhere stranded. Otele uses a wide range of materials, including literature, art, and archaeology, but other sources such as letters, diaries, or government documents, would have added additional depth and richness to the book. Given the broad scope of her work, the absence of these gives a feeling that some subjects could benefit from more in-depth analysis and explanation.

Resistance and Liberation Movements

The resistance and liberation movements of the African diaspora are part of a larger story of African resistance against enslavement and colonialism. A desire for freedom, dignity, and equality drove these movements into action. They took many forms, from organized rebellions and uprisings to cultural resistance and acts of everyday defiance.

"The Black Civil Rights Movement in America from 1950s to 1960s," by He Yufeng and Zhu Rui,[16] is a research paper that explores the broader resistance movement of the African Diaspora through the Black civil rights movement in the United States during the mid twentieth century. The authors provide an overview of the key events, actors, and ideas that shaped the movement, and they examine the movement's impact on American society and politics. The

---

15   Otele, *African Europeans*.

16   He Yufeng and Zhu Rui, "The Black civil rights movement in America from 1950s to 1960s," in *2021 4th International Conference on Humanities Education and Social Sciences (ICHESS 2021)*, (Dordrecht: Atlantis Press, 2021), 1058–1065.

authors begin by exploring the historical context of the Black civil rights movement, including the legacies of slavery and Jim Crow segregation.[17] Then, they provide a chronological overview of the movement, highlighting key events such as the Montgomery bus boycott,[18] the Greensboro sit-ins,[19] the Freedom Rides,[20] and the March on Washington.[21] The authors also examine the role of key leaders and organizations, including Martin Luther King, Jr., the Student Nonviolent Coordinating Committee and the Southern Christian Leadership Conference. The authors also explore how American society and politics were affected by the Black civil rights movement. They argue that the movement successfully advanced the cause of civil rights and equality for African Americans, but these gains were limited by continued resistance from segregationist forces and the persistence of structural racism in American society.

"The Influence of the Civil Rights and Black Power Movement in Canada,"[22] by Agnes Calliste, is another research article that explores how the US Civil Rights and Black Power movements affected Black Canadians. Calliste argues that movements in the United States had a profound influence on Black Canadians, inspiring similar movements for social justice and equality in Canada. The article begins by situating the Civil Rights and Black Power movements within a broader context of Black struggles for freedom and equality in North America. Calliste then provides a detailed overview of these movements influencing Black Canadians, including the rise of Black activism and political consciousness, the development of Black cultural expression, and the growth of Black-led organizations and movements. The US movements provided inspiration that led to the growth of Black political activism in Canada, along with cultural expressions and community organizing.

Calliste highlights how Black leaders and organizations, such as the Black United Front[23] and the Congress of Black Women, shaped the development of the Black Power movement in Canada. Her article also explores the limitations and challenges faced by Black Canadians in their struggles for social justice and

---

[17] Brian Norman, *Neo-Segregation Narratives: Jim Crow in Post-Civil Rights American Literature* (Athens: University of Georgia Press, 2010).

[18] Randall Kennedy, "Martin Luther King's constitution: A legal history of the Montgomery bus boycott," *The Yale Law Journal* 98 (1988): 999.

[19] Rebekah J. Kowal, "Staging the Greensboro sit-ins," *The Drama Review* 48, 4 (2004): 135–154.

[20] James Peck, *Freedom Ride* (New York: Simon and Schuster, 1962).

[21] William P. Jones, *The March on Washington: Jobs, Freedom, and the Forgotten History of Civil Rights* (New York: W. W. Norton, 2013).

[22] Agnes Calliste, "The influence of the civil rights and Black power movement in Canada," *Race, Gender & Class* 2, 3 (1995): 123–139.

[23] Cicero Alvin Hughes, *Toward a Black United Front: The National Negro Congress Movement* (Athens: Ohio University Press, 1982).

equality. She argues that Canada's Black Power movement faced significant obstacles, including racism, discrimination, limited access to political power, and a lack of resources. Despite these challenges, Canada's Black Power movement was instrumental in advancing the cause of Black freedom and equality in the country.

"The Influence of the Civil Rights and Black Power Movement in Canada" is a valuable contribution to the study of Black struggles for freedom and equality in North America. Calliste provides a detailed analysis of how the Civil Rights and Black Power movements impacted Black Canadians, and she offers insights into the challenges and limitations that Black Canadians face in their ongoing struggle for justice and equality. However, Calliste's article focuses exclusively on the influence of US Civil Rights and Black Power movements on Black Canadians, which limits its ability to provide a full understanding of these movements' broader context and impact. The article does not consider the influence of other political and social movements that shaped Black activism and political consciousness in Canada. Rather, it provides a detailed overview of the Civil Rights and Black Power movements, but it does not fully consider how other historical events and movements influenced the development of Black activism in Canada. The article omits the impacts of the Underground Railroad,[24] the abolitionist movement,[25] and World Wars I and II on Black activism in Canada.

Moreover, Calliste's article focuses exclusively on Canada, with no provision of a comparative analysis of the impact of the Civil Rights and Black Power movements in other countries. It does not consider how the Civil Rights and Black Power movements influenced Black populations in other parts of the world, such as Africa or the Caribbean. Although the article ends its analysis in the late 1960s, the Civil Rights and Black Power movements continued to evolve and impact North American society and politics in the decades that followed.

"Pan-Africanism and 'Pan-Africanism': Some Historical Notes,"[26] a research article by George Shepperson, is an exploration of Pan-Africanism's historical roots and conceptual evolution. He provides a critical analysis of Pan-Africanism's origins and development, arguing that the term has taken on different meanings and interpretations over time. Shepperson begins with a brief overview of the historical context in which Pan-Africanism emerged. He notes that the term was first used in the late nineteenth century to reference the growing sense of solidarity and

---

[24] Matthew Clavin, "Making freedom: The Underground Railroad and the politics of slavery," *Civil War Book Review* 16, 1 (2014): Article 17.

[25] Claudine L. Ferrell, *The Abolitionist Movement* (Santa Barbara: Greenwood, 2006).

[26] George Shepperson, "Pan-Africanism and 'Pan-Africanism': Some historical notes," *Phylon* 23, 4 (1962): 346–358.

connection between people of African descent around the world. His detailed analysis of Pan-Africanism's evolution as a concept includes its connection with anti-colonial and anti-imperialist movements in the twentieth century.

Shepperson asserts that the concept of Pan-Africanism has assumed different meanings and interpretations over time. Some early Pan-Africanists promoted a sense of unity and solidarity among all people of African descent, and others saw Pan-Africanism as a movement to support anti-colonial and anti-imperialist struggles. Shepperson critiques the limitations of some early Pan-Africanist movements, such as their lack of attention to the diversity of the African Diaspora and their limited focus on political and economic struggles. He argues that despite these limitations, the concept of Pan-Africanism remains an important and influential idea, shaping the development of Black political activism and cultural expression around the world.

Shepperson's article focuses on the early history of Pan-Africanism from the late nineteenth century to the mid twentieth century. It does not provide a comprehensive analysis of the concept's evolution and development in the decades that followed, which falls short of fully considering the broader Pan-Africanist movement's diversity of perspectives and interpretations. Although his article provides a general overview of Pan-Africanism's development, it does not consider regional variations and differences that occurred in locations such as Africa, the Caribbean, and the Americas. In focusing on the political and economic dimensions of Pan-Africanism, the article pays limited attention to cultural expressions. It does not fully consider the role of cultural influences and creative forms of expression, such as literature, music, and art, in shaping Pan-Africanism's development.

What is African Diaspora in the Modern World?

In *African Europeans* Olivette Otele reveals a part of history that many have overlooked. *African Europeans* is an important book on Black populations in Europe. Her book fills gaps in the historical narrative by highlighting overlooked or erased stories and contributions from Black people in Europe. Otele's book dives straight into an account of African enslavement and the construct of the Negro. This information remains relevant to contemporary events, such as the Black Lives Matter (BLM) protests and conversations around slavery, racism, and critical race theory. The BLM movement began in 2013 as a response to the killing of Trayvon Martin, a seventeen-year-old African-American student. Since then, the movement has attained global momentum, resonating with Black people around the world. The movement has grown in countries like South Africa, which has not fully healed from apartheid, and in Western European countries that are confronting their colonial past.

Otele's book provides historical context for present-day issues addressed by the BLM movement. She argues that Black lives are undervalued, that race has been used to justify Blacks being controlled by others, and it has normalized the loss of Black lives. Otele points to the 1738 law in France that forbade Blacks from marrying. Soon after, a special police unit was created to monitor the number of Blacks in the country, regarded as enslaved people without freedom. These actions demonstrate how Black lives were devalued in Europe, and their oppression was normalized.

African Europeans critiques the idea of African exceptionalism. Otele maintains that "Africans who were valuable enough to be remembered were those who had been deemed exceptional," thus, leading to the acknowledgment of a few. The book highlights five major patterns that define racial minorities in Europe: infantilization, paternalization, exoticism, bestiality, and exceptionalism. These patterns from the past remain applicable today. The book describes historical narratives of Africans needing to be domesticated so that the Europeans around them could feel safe. Blacks were kept away from Europe for similar reasons. Otele notes that such narratives can be seen in current discussions about refugees and irregular migrants in Europe, discussing refugee and migrant testimonies that show how they are viewed as threats and treated as subhuman.

The African Diaspora faces a mix of challenges and opportunities in the modern world. On the one hand, members of the diaspora continue to face systemic racism and discrimination, especially in countries where they are in the minority. This can lead to difficulties accessing education, employment, and housing opportunities, along with higher rates of poverty and incarceration. On the other hand, many members of the African Diaspora have achieved great success, making significant contributions to local and global societies. In business, politics, and the arts, individuals of African descent have demonstrated their talent and resilience in the face of adversity. The diaspora also has a strong sense of community and cultural identity that transcends borders, which has led to the creation of vibrant, supportive networks around the world. Overall, the African Diaspora remains a diverse and dynamic community that continues to wield significant influence in the twenty-first century.

Conclusion

The African Diaspora's history is a complex and frequently tragic tale of displacement, oppression, and resilience. The transatlantic slave trade began in the sixteenth century and lasted for more than three centuries, constituting the largest forced migration in world history. The consequences were enormous. Slavery's legacy continues to shape the global experiences of people of African descent who face ongoing discrimination and inequality in many countries.

Despite these challenges, the African Diaspora's rich cultural heritage shows creativity, resilience, and ability to adapt to new circumstances. People of African descent have created vibrant, dynamic communities that enrich the cultures, music, art, food, and religions of their adopted countries. The concept of an overlapping diaspora highlights the complex and layered identities of people of African descent, underscoring the importance of recognizing and valuing the diversity of their experiences and perspectives.

In an interconnected world, it is important to understand and appreciate the history of the African diaspora. By reflecting on the past, we can gain a deeper appreciation for the sacrifices and struggles of those who came before us, and we can be inspired to work for a more just and equitable future for all people, regardless of their background. The history of the African Diaspora is one of tragedy, perseverance, and triumph, and it reminds us of the importance of remembering our shared history and working toward a better future for all.

2 Interrogating the Conception and Construction of African Diaspora History

Introduction

The African Diaspora's history dates back to the origins of humanity. There have been several controversies regarding those origins, but a consensus holds that Africans have been migrating for more than 100,000 years.[27] In their travels and voyages, Africans transform the world in many ways, and they are transformed themselves. Like the history of Africa itself, the African Diaspora includes different perspectives and accommodates diverse scholarly approaches. Although the African continent's origins have been the subject of many studies, the African Diaspora has attracted marginal attention.

The recent increase in research focused on the African Diaspora has been promising; it is an area of inquiry that seeks to uncover the dynamics, construction, and conception of Africans. However, the field not only lacks a comprehensive historical perspective to put the subject into context but is also challenged by methodological vagueness and romantic condescension. Even with these shortcomings, it has attracted an increasing amount of attention, which is evident in the

---

[27] Palmer, "The African Diaspora," 56–59.

growing number of conferences, specialists, scholars, book prizes, Ph.D. programs, and courses focused on the African Diaspora.

Although the concept of an "African Diaspora" became commonly used in the early 1960s, it has existed since the nineteenth century. However, the idea has yet to be comprehensively and systematically defined. Different controversies surround the actual meaning of the concept. Some use the term to describe individuals of African origin who have left the continental territory of their ancestors, and others simply use the term to discuss Africans abroad. Others view the idea as synonymous with a recently introduced topic: the "Black Atlantic." The truth is that whenever the concept of diaspora surfaces, it is not restricted to the continent of Africa.

History suggests that the settlement of the Americas was driven by migration from Asia, although it occurred 15,000 to 20,000 years ago when migrants traveled across the Bering Strait to inhabit North America, South America, and the Caribbean islands.[28] There is a Jewish Diaspora, which started around 5,000 years ago, and it is often regarded as the most widely studied phenomenon since the beginning of Diasporan studies.[29] There was a Diasporic migration, driven by cultural and religious motives among Muslims in the eighth century, which brought Islamic tenets and doctrines into various parts of Asia, Europe, and Africa. Europeans have also engaged in diasporic movement – in the fifteenth century, they infiltrated the continent of Africa and drove the dispersal of Africans throughout the world.

The term "diaspora" can be examined both culturally and historically. Although it is popularly used to refer to Jewish populations scattered across the West, the word's origin comes from the Greek term for "dispersal." Its meaning in modern Black culture can be traced to Psalms Chapter 68, Verse 31 in the Old Testament, which states, "Ethiopia shall soon stretch out her hands unto God." To African Americans, this biblical excerpt clearly describes the Black race and its search for freedom. Early historical studies focused on the global movement of the Black race driven by colonialism, racism, and injustice, along with Africa's general role in the development of the modern world.

Diaspora can be conceived as both a condition and a process. It is a process because it can constantly be imagined through political thoughts, struggles, and cultural production while being reimagined through travel, migration, and movement.[30] It is a condition because it is closely connected to the process of

---

[28] Colin A. Palmer, "Defining and studying the modern African Diaspora," *The Journal of Negro History* 85, 1–2 (2000): 27–32.

[29] Paul Tiyambe Zeleza, "Rewriting the African Diaspora: Beyond the Black Atlantic," *African Affairs* 104, 414 (2005): 35–68.

[30] Colin A. Palmer, "Social Movements in the African Diaspora during the Twentieth Century," Course Content, (Graduate School of the City University of New York, 1997).

being made and remade. The African Diaspora itself is reflected in world hierarchies of race and gender, which have been revised and reconstructed across several divisions, barriers, and national boundaries. These barriers include: restrictions placed on the process of acquiring citizenship in countries that claim to uphold the principles and rules of democracy;[31] limits placed on cultural values that result in the attribution of negative values to indigenous territory while that territory's positive and expressive values are embraced and appropriated, especially for commercial and political purposes; economic boundaries imposed to make the indigenous economies untenable through the construction of a persistent colonial economy and a global market;[32] imperial boundaries placed on industrial production;[33] and social boundaries, such as "Jim Crow" restrictions, that create social systems where access to specific privileges are based on gender and race, regardless of whether the society is open or segregated.[34]

The concept of diaspora is bordered by discontinuities and differences. It consists of a group's lived experiences that are shaped by alienation and different binary associations like alien/native. It also includes the "dispersal from a homeland, often by violent forces, the making of a memory and a vision of that homeland, marginalization in the new location, a commitment to the maintenance or restoration of the homeland, and desire for return and a continuing relationship and identity with the homeland that shapes the consciousness and solidarity of a group."[35]

According to Palmer, the African Diaspora, in modern context, refers to the global community of people of African descent who are bonded by histories and experiences that include racial oppression, by the social, cultural, and emotional connections they share to their ancestral continent, and their continued struggles in constructing and shaping their identities.[36] The conception and construction of the African Diaspora's history is necessary to fully understand the African Diaspora itself. This study pursues that understanding through historiographies of related subjects, including the conception of the origins of the African Diaspora, the historical construction of the African Diaspora's past and the dominant narrative of the African Diaspora's history.

---

[31] Palmer, "Social Movements in the African Diaspora during the Twentieth Century."
[32] Thomas Clive, *The Poor and the Powerless: Economic Policy and Change in the Caribbean* (London: Latin America Bureau, 1988).
[33] Clive, *The Poor and the Powerless*.
[34] International Labour Organization (ILO), *Plantation Workers: Conditions of Work and Standards of Living* (Geneva: International Labour Office, 1966).
[35] Patterson and Kelley, "Unfinished migrations," 15.
[36] Palmer, "Social Movements in the African Diaspora during the Twentieth Century."

Understanding the Conception of the Origins of the African Diaspora

Before the emergence of the phenomenon currently known as the Atlantic Diaspora, which began in the fourteenth century, there had been earlier African migrations, particularly to the Indian Ocean. This movement dates back to the fifth century, and it consisted of soldiers, merchants, and sailors, unlike more recent migrations that were driven by slavery.[37] The origins of the modern African Diaspora began with earlier movements of both the free and enslaved Africans across the Indian Ocean, the Red Sea, and the Mediterranean Sea. The transatlantic slave trade is an integral part of the modern African Diaspora; it disrupted and displaced countless people of African descent, placing them in various worlds that were new and different from their indigenous territories. The work of Africans on plantations and providing other commercial services was a major component of industrial developments that characterized the Americas between the fifteenth and nineteenth centuries.[38]

Contextual sources of the African Diaspora are the border transgressions that resulted from Euro-American imperialism, along with the extraction and exploitation of physical and human resources. European modernity was a major cultural focus after triangular trade routes were established via the "Middle Course."[39] Colonialism and slavery were the bedrock of development in Europe and other continents populated by people of African descent, which suggests that the recent idea of globalization and its economic objectives will remain reliant on African labor.

Globalization has always depended on African labor; European modernity gave Europeans the economic and political power necessary to control global resources with preexisting institutions. Through forced and free migrations, Africans moved to Asia, Europe, and the Americas while maintaining and creating unique sociocultural practices in these different societies – Africans became global inhabitants. The migration of Africans to various parts of the world rendered them vulnerable and subjected them to dispossession and subordination.[40] This unhealthy state of being, which characterized the existence and lives of these Africans, has driven many scholars to study the origins of African Diasporic movements. Detailed analysis and criticism of these studies and works can provide a more comprehensive understanding of the subject.

---

[37] Carole Davies, (ed.), *Encyclopedia of the African Diaspora: Origins, Experiences, and Culture*, Vol. 1 (Santa Barbara: ABC-Clio, 2008).

[38] Palmer, "Defining and studying the modern African Diaspora," 27–32.

[39] Davies, (ed.), *Encyclopedia of the African Diaspora*.

[40] Ben Vinson, "Introduction: African (Black) Diaspora history, Latin American history 1," *The Americas* 63, 1 (2006): 1–18.

Various historians chose to uncover the conception of the origins of the African Diaspora, but Colin Palmer[41] and Joseph Harris[42] have offered perspectives that made immense contributions to the study. Other significant contributions were made by historians Gwendolyn Midlo Hall[43] and Michael Gomez.[44]

Colin Palmer's "Defining and Studying the Modern African Diaspora" is a well-detailed and rich account of historical developments on the continent of Africa and among its inhabitants, accurately recounting the origins of diasporic movements. Palmer identifies diaspora as a multifaceted concept before expounding on the nature and scope of each facet. His work emphasizes religious and continental movements that continue across centuries – Palmer asserts that these movements could be considered diasporic streams that are dissimilar in various ways, such as nature, direction, and timing. He maintains that the diasporic movement of Africa's people is neither singular nor a monolithic diasporic community. Palmer's work divides African diasporic movements into five major streams based on time and motivating factors.

Palmer explains that the first diasporic stream occurred around 100,000 years ago. It is the oldest and earliest such movement, and debates have established its validity as a starting point for the dispersal of Africans and their settling in other parts of the world. The study of diasporic history entails a study of early human beings, and Palmer asserts that this first stream of the African Diaspora should be carefully examined as an integral part of its history. His idea has been challenged by other scholars who argue that the first stream lacks the characteristic features of subsequent movements and settlements; it remains a controversial issue.

The movement of Bantu-speaking people to the Indian Ocean and other parts of the African continent, which took place around 3,000 B.C.E, is the second diasporic stream. Palmer identifies a third stream, which was driven by commercial interests starting in the fifth century. This involved the movement of merchants, traders, and slaves to areas that offered greater economic opportunities. These migrants found settlements in Asia, the Middle East, and Europe. The texture, capacity, and pace of the third diasporic stream was uneven, which is why the seventh-century slave trade driven by Muslims – which largely involved migrations of a new scope and intensity – was not considered a new diasporic stream.

---

[41] Palmer, "The African Diaspora," 56–65.

[42] Joseph E. Harris, (ed.), *Global Dimensions of the African Diaspora*, 2nd ed., (Washington, DC: Howard University Press, 1993).

[43] Gwendolyn Midlo Hall, *Slavery and African Ethnicities in the Americas: Restoring the Links* (Chapel Hill: University of North Carolina Press, 2005).

[44] Michael A. Gomez, (ed.), *Diasporic Africa: A Reader* (New York: New York University Press, 2006); and Michael A. Gomez, *Reversing Sail: A History of the African Diaspora*(New York: Cambridge University Press, 2005).

The third diasporic movement continued for years, establishing communities of African descent in European countries that included Italy, Spain, and Portugal, along with settlements in the Middle East and Asian territories such as India. This happened several centuries before Christopher Columbus crossed the Atlantic. Palmer cites Frank Snowden, a researcher in the field of African history, who states that the "exact number of Ethiopians who entered the Greco-Roman world as a result of military, diplomatic, and commercial activity is difficult to determine and that all the evidence suggests a sizable Ethiopian element, especially in the population of the Roman world."[45] Individuals who would be considered Black Africans were previously described as Ethiopians. According to Palmer, the first through third diasporic streams are considered the pre-contemporary African Diaspora.

Palmer associates the fourth diasporic stream with the fifteenth-century transatlantic slave trade, and it is the most widely studied African diasporic movement in the present day. It marked the beginning of a global trade in humans, moving more than 200,000 Africans to different countries and societies in Europe. Around 12 million Africans were also traded to the Americas.

The fifth diasporic stream began after the abolition of slavery, starting in the nineteenth century and continuing into the present. It involves the movement and resettlement of people of African descent in different societies. When compared with pre-contemporary diasporic streams, Palmer finds these subsequent diasporic streams to be characterized by the constant resistance and grave racial oppression that is associated with the modern African Diaspora. Each of the five diasporic streams involves major movements of Africans within and outside the continent.

Palmer also considers the work of other scholars and African historians, especially the ideas popularized by Paul Gilroy. He cautions that Gilroy's idea of the modern African Diaspora as directly synonymous with the term "Black Atlantic" requires greater clarification. Palmer notes that the "Black Atlantic" appellation can exclude communities not located in the Atlantic basin, such as those in the Indian Ocean. The term also ignores fundamental distinctions between the historical experiences of South Atlantic and North Atlantic residents. Before such a label can be fully embraced, Palmer asserts that scholars and historians must resist attempts to fuse or homogenize historical narratives from residents whose experiences are built around an ocean that symbolizes their ancestral toils and travails. He also opposes the term "Plantation America"

---

[45] Frank M. Snowden Jr., *Blacks in Antiquity: Ethiopians in the Greco-Roman World* (Cambridge, MA: Harvard University Press, 1970), 184.

to describe individuals of African descent because it renders Black people invisible and characterizes them through an economic arrangement or system.

Palmer's "Defining and Studying the Modern African Diaspora" provides a complete analysis of the African Diaspora's origins and discusses major developments that followed the dispersal of Africans across the world. However, Palmer does not examine the impact of each diasporic stream on people of African descent and the communities that received them. The work is not substantive enough to evaluate the inhumane conditions to which Africans were subjected during the diasporic movements, especially through the transatlantic slave trade. Palmer explains the inappropriateness of terms such as "Plantation American" and "Black Atlantic" in his closing paragraphs, but the reader is left without much insight into the conditions that led to their conception. Further elaboration could have alerted readers to the lack of such concepts in the African Diaspora's historical developments.

Joseph Harris also made significant contributions to the conception of the origin of the African Diaspora in *Global Dimensions of the African Diaspora*. His voluminous, well-detailed description and analysis of the African Diaspora ranges from theories surrounding the concept of diaspora to fundamental case studies. Harris's book discusses the subject of the African Diaspora from an "omniscient point of view," providing all the facts and details without bias and expanding his view of the African Diaspora beyond the conventional scope of the Atlantic Diaspora.[46] Harris explains the various ways in which people of African descent were required to live simultaneously as citizens of other nations and as children of Africa. Although the book illustrates diasporic movements in many parts of the world, it does not provide an extensive explanation regarding the wider significance of the African Diaspora. Its emphasis on migrations to Europe and the Americas means that other destinations receive considerably less coverage.[47]

Mirroring the Historical Construction of African Diaspora History

The term "diaspora" has evolved over the years to become a global phrase attracting public and critical discourses. Its usage has become increasingly popular among individuals and scholars, especially those in the fields of history and African studies. It is often explored alongside phenomena such as transnationalism and globalization, but unlike these other concepts, diaspora actively contests the yet-to-be-resolved identities of race and nations along with the

---

[46] Harris, *Global Dimensions of the African Diaspora*.
[47] Ibrahim K. Sundiata, "State formation and trade: The rise and fall of the Bubi polity, c. 1840–1910," *The International Journal of African Historical Studies* 27, 3 (1994): 662–663.

gender and class hierarchies that bedevil different diasporic streams and movements.[48] Studies of diaspora also seek to acknowledge, value, and honor the different perspectives, experiences, and abilities of individuals from different backgrounds, identities, and experiences. From Orlando Patterson's point of view, diaspora remains a setting of social death under the evocative nature of slavery, where booming investments are geared toward creating new possibilities that presage a globalized future for every nation of the world.[49]

News and images of violently displaced refugees and boat people from Somalia and Vietnam have recently become regular trends on television and the internet. However, the research conducted on diaspora-related issues, including Paul Gilroy's *The Black Atlantic: Modernity and Double Consciousness*, has earned recognition for acutely focusing on diasporic agency and originality.[50] With the help of such works, readers and the general African public are provided an alternative to historical stories of relentless diasporic mimicry, flattery, and victimization that surround African diasporic movements. These studies also venerate the cosmopolitan scholars and historians who have devoted their time and resources to producing such work.

There remains a limited understanding of the African Diaspora as a subject in spite of the growing scholarship on it. In addition to the conceptual difficulties surrounding the meaning and ideal definition of diaspora, and the African Diaspora in particular, there is also an undue focus on the American stream of the African Diaspora – also considered to be the Anglophone or Atlantic Diaspora. This propensity to privilege the Americas is reflected in Gilroy's work.

Gilroy's *The Black Atlantic* is a reliable point of reference for the historical construction of the African Diaspora's history. Gilroy's book is less recognized for its contributions to the study of the economic, cultural, social, and political relations among the major components of the Atlantic world – the interrelated systems of Europe, the Americas, and Africa – because it fails to offer comprehensive details about the nature and developments of these systems. However, the book's influence and authority draws from its focus on the African-American diaspora and its anti-nationalistic ideological and theoretical politics.

At the initial publication of *The Black Atlantic*, it was recognized as a world-class analysis that resonated with the anti-nationalistic campaigns of postcolonialism, post-structuralism, and postmodernism. It also addressed subjects that

---

[48] Judith Byfield, "Rethinking the African Diaspora," *African Studies Review* 43, 1 (2000): 1–9.

[49] Orlando Patterson, *Slavery and Social Death: A Comparative Study* (Cambridge, MA: Harvard University Press, 1982).

[50] Paul Gilroy, *The Black Atlantic: Modernity and Double Consciousness* (Cambridge, MA: Harvard University Press, 1993).

included the proliferating controversies surrounding African-American diaspora studies that were motivated by broader struggles over affirmative action and the Afrocentric model. The intellectual capacity of *The Black Atlantic* triggered a continuous search for recent analytics in the American academy.

Multiple themes are presented in *The Black Atlantic*, but they center on the propensity to disintegrate the Black race, demonstrating its contemporary nature, mutability, and fluidity while separating it from any African presence or essence.[51] The book also clarifies how Black Atlantic cultural identities emerged through the intercultural and international systems of diasporic events. Gilroy presents this emergence as an ideal reaction to the adverse effects of racism and transoceanic exchanges, generating mixed and creolized experiences, cultural artifacts, and ideas such as music and other complementary ways of life.

Although it made contributions to cultural and diasporic studies, Gilroy's book has also been criticized for several reasons. The book mirrors the historical construction of the African Diaspora's history, but it simplifies the African-American experience along with African connections and roles in its aggregate reflection and memory.[52] Despite its stated sensitivity to gender and gender-related issues, *The Black Atlantic* remains largely androcentric, crediting male figures for the evolution of Atlantic Blackness and modernity.

Another shortcoming of Gilroy's book is that it makes the racialized "ethnic" experiences, which a large number of African Americans endured, into a universal identity, asserting that every part of the Caribbean Islands was occupied by similar people of African descent. Although it works to create a multicultural or Black Atlantic, the book has been faulted for its postmodernist fears regarding essentialism and strategic or imaginary systems.[53] Instead of expounding on the connections and relationships among the many Black diasporic cultures and histories, the ideas presented in the book foreclose such relationships. These overlooked possibilities, especially between African and Anglophone cultures, extend to the Portuguese-speaking diasporic population of Brazil, which is one of the most significant in the Anglophone world.

Gilroy's work also displays modernity as the fundamental rationale for the Black Atlantic critique, which omits inquiries that relate to capitalism and imperialism.[54] Gilroy's *The Black Atlantic* remains ironic in the present day.

---

[51] Zeleza, "Rewriting the African Diaspora," 41.

[52] Michael Echeruo, "An African Diaspora: The ontological project," in Isidore Okpewho and Nkiru Nzegwu, (eds.), *The New African Diaspora* (Bloomington: Indiana University Press, 2001), 3–18.

[53] Ntongela Masilela, "'The Black Atlantic' and African modernity in South Africa," *Research in African Literatures* 27, 4 (1996), 88–96.

[54] Laura Chrisman, "Rethinking Black Atlanticism," *Black Scholar* 30, 3/4 (2000): 12–17.

Although it frowns at the descriptive exceptionalism of African Americans – seeking to emphasize the awareness across every part of Europe that has been popularized by African-American icons such as Richard Wright[55] and W.E.B Du Bois[56] – the book is frequently referenced as a portrayal of the myopia and self-referential qualities of the Americas. However, the African Diaspora is more expressive and ready to embrace members of other communities, which makes the irony more of a tribute than a criticism. This is further reflected in the rich ideas of Blackness and African Diaspora that are in sharp contrast to the hegemony of the United States' imperialism. Strong, complex, and sometimes contradictory connections have been drawn between the African Diaspora in the United Kingdom and in the United States, which is particularly evident in the evolution of Black modernities. This is similar to the connections and relationships that exist between Africans and their African-American counterparts.

The critique of myopic self-referentialism in *The Black Atlantic* was supported by Ntongela Masilela, Robert Trent Vinson, and Amanda Kemp.[57] Vinson and Kemp assert that the expressive cultural practices constituting the principal attributes of African Americans and others in the African Diaspora – such as language, mode of dressing, choice of dress, and music – circulated through the transatlantic territories. This circulation is reliable evidence of African cosmopolitanism adopted as a practical instrument in an incredibly racialized society; it divorces modernity from whiteness through the reversal and mockery of the "racial era" of "white modernity" that kept people of African descent locked in an uncivilized, static state.[58]

Staying Power, Black London and *Africans in Britain* are three of the most famous historical narratives of the British African Diaspora history, by Peter Fryer,[59] Gretchen H. Gerzina[60], and David Killingray,[61] respectively. These works reflect the overwhelming popularity of African-American culture,[62] and Laura Chrisman emphasizes this notion:

---

[55] Richard Wright, "Blueprint for negro writing," in Winston Napier, (ed.), *African American Literary Theory: A Reader* (New York: New York University Press, 2000), 45–53.

[56] W. E. B Du Bois, *The Oxford WEB Du Bois*, vol. 1, The Suppression of the African Slave-Trade to the United States of America 1638–1870 (Oxford: Oxford University Press, 2007).

[57] Masilela, "'The Black Atlantic' and African modernity in South Africa."

[58] Amanda Kemp and Robert Trent Vinson, "Professor James Thaele, American Negroes, and modernity in 1920s segregationist South Africa," *African Studies Review* 43, 1 (2000): 14.

[59] Peter Fryer, *Staying Power: The History of Black People in Britain* (Edmonton: University of Alberta, 1984).

[60] Gretchen Holbrook Gerzina, *Black London: Life before Emancipation* (New Brunswick: Rutgers University Press, 1995).

[61] David Killingray, (ed.), *Africans in Britain* (Oxfordshire: Routledge, 2012).

[62] Peter Fryer, *Staying Power: The History of Black People in Britain* (London: Pluto, 1984); Gerzina, *Black London*; and Killingray, *Africans in Britain*.

> I am arguing for new methods that articulate a version of black Atlanticism that does not contract African America, or the African diaspora, as a sovereign class or icon of modernity that then gets imposed upon African populations. If we are to retain the language of black modernity in our analyses – and I think we should – we need to open up its multiple geographical, economic, philosophical and aesthetic constituents rather than using it as a singular term for a New World act of cultural self-fashioning.[63]

These works pluralize and historicize the African Diaspora, tracing its diverse identifications and identities back to the continent of Africa. Even the occasional incapacity to effectively execute this mapping surpasses the phenomenon of racial essentialism underscored by Gilroy's *The Black Atlantic*. Gilroy has dedicated substantial time and resources to analyzing the harms of "raciology," or the ideas commonly described as the "fictions" of Blackness, in a vain attempt to create a world that will eventually become what Toni Morrison describes as "raceless or unraced by assertion."[64]

Interrogating the Dominant Narrative of African Diaspora History

Butler applies her rich knowledge of African Diaspora history in Brazil to emphasize that the conceptualization of diaspora is not complete unless it underscores the various phases of diasporization and embraces the reality of multiple identities. Her ideas provide an essential outline of the subject's five simple dimensions. These include (1) the conditions and purpose of the dispersal, (2) the connection and relationship with the host territory, (3) the connection and relationship with the homeland, (4) comparative study and research on various diasporas, and (5) the interconnections and associations within the diaspora groups.[65]

Robin Cohen complements Butler's analysis by suggesting that certain characteristics qualify a system as a diaspora. Cohen identifies nine unique characteristics from which a suggestive schema can be established, creating distinctions among the many varieties of diasporic movements. These distinctions led to the Caribbean transfers being identified as a "cultural diaspora," Chinese and Lebanese movements identified as "trade diasporas," British migration being identified as the "imperial diaspora," and Indian settlement identified as "labour diasporas." The situations of Africans and Armenians are described as "victim diasporas."

Cohen's groupings are easily identifiable, and they are not mutually exclusive. It is interesting that the African Diaspora – unlike other systems that are

---

[63] Chrisman, "Rethinking Black Atlanticism." 38.

[64] Toni Morrison, *Playing in the Dark: Whiteness and the Literary Imagination* (New York: Vintage, 1992), 46.

[65] Kim Butler, "Brazilian abolition in Afro-Atlantic context," *African Studies Review* 43, 1 (2000): 127.

described by ethnic, national or even ideological terms – is simply described as African. This occurs regardless of whether the identity of the referent is clear, either spatially or racially. The description of the African Diaspora as "Black" is another divergence from other diaspora systems or categories, which are rarely named after color. The description can be politically contested, but the fact remains that other diaspora categories are named after national, ethnic, religious, or linguistic properties. Outside of the contextual overview of the African Diaspora's nature and its history, there are different narratives surrounding the history of the African Diaspora itself. Many historians and intellectuals have popularized the dominant narrative on this subject.

The racialization and homogenization of people of African descent have gained popularity and acceptance in recent academic discourse, both within and beyond the continent. This trend is encouraged by scholars who are less willing to unravel the astonishing features of the African Diaspora or to build an independent, Pan-African solidarity. In this light, Edward Alpers writes in "The African Diaspora in the Indian Ocean: A Comparative Perspective" that the racialization and homogenization of the African Diaspora is:

> based entirely upon the Atlantic experience of forced migration, which is a phenomenon spanning the 16th–19th centuries ... The Indian Ocean setting complicates this situation by having experienced both a much longer history of forced migration ... as well as a more modest tradition of free labour migration that muddies the waters.[66]

In "Rewriting the African Diaspora: Beyond the Black Atlantic," Paul Zeleza added that trade migrations and free labor remained the defining features of African Diasporic waves during the post-slavery era.[67] From the twentieth century onwards, Zeleza observes that the new African Diaspora triggered continuous, gradually increasing migrations. He attempts a broader overview of diaspora as a topic to make his narrative comprehensive; Zeleza considers diaspora to be a discourse, space, condition, and process. Along with other scholars in the field, he considers the modern implications of the African Diaspora, including the severe brain drain that has left the continent in a state of perpetual underdevelopment. Rather than delve into the historical background of the African Diaspora, Zeleza explores "modern historical streams of the global African diaspora."[68] Prior to Zeleza's work, several books and articles focused on expounding similar ideas, but a full account of the African

---

[66] Edward Alpers, "The African Diaspora in the Indian Ocean: A comparative perspective," in Shihan Jayasuriya and Richard Pankhurst, (eds.), *The African Diaspora in the Indian Ocean* (Trenton: Africa World Press, 2003), 21–22.

[67] Zeleza, "Rewriting the African Diaspora," 35–68.

[68] Zeleza, "Rewriting the African Diaspora," 43.

Diaspora's global dimensions has not been covered in a single study. Neither the intriguing *The Black Diaspora: Five Centuries of Black Experience Outside Africa* by Ronald Segal[69] nor the celebrated work of Joseph Harris[70] provide complete assessments of the subject's global implications.[71] Instead, efforts have described the history and development of the Atlantic world, which only constitutes part of a complex whole. This sharply contrasts with the material obtainable on the Mediterranean and Indian Ocean Diasporas. The amount of literature on these other diasporas is constantly increasing, reflected in texts such as *The African Diaspora in the Mediterranean Lands of Islam*,[72] by Eve Trout Powell and John Hunwick[73] and *The African Diaspora in the Indian Ocean* by Richard Pankhurst and Shihan de Jayasuriya.[74]

Because the diaspora categories and systems discussed in these texts involve integral parts of the African continent, they encounter the same definitional problem as other literature addressing the African Diaspora. Among the eight chapters composing Pankhurst and Jayasuriya's *The African Diaspora in the Indian Ocean*,[75] only three focus on India and Sri Lanka. The remaining chapters discuss the Indian Ocean islands of Mauritius, Réunion, and Madagascar. One of the authors explains this problem:

> The Indian Ocean Islands that are considered in this paper are usually classified geographically as African islands … In the geographical sense then the 'African Diaspora' would be an intra-African one: from the continent to its offshore islands so to speak.[76]

The racialized diminishment and categorization of Africa is even more evident in the work of Powell and Hunwick. Hunwick states:

> The compartmentalization of Africa into zones that are treated as 'Middle East' and 'Africa' is a legacy of Orientalism and colonialism. North Africa, including Egypt, is usually seen as forming part of the Middle East, though Middle East experts are not generally keen to venture farther west than the confines of Egypt.

---

[69] Ronald Segal, *The Black Diaspora: Five Centuries of the Black Experience Outside Africa* (New York: Farrar, Straus and Giroux, 1995).

[70] Harris, *Global Dimensions of the African Diaspora.*

[71] Segal, *The Black Diaspora*; and Harris, *Global Dimensions of the African Diaspora.*

[72] John Hunwick and Eve Troutt Powell, *The African Diaspora in the Mediterranean Lands of Islam* (Princeton: Markus Wiener, 2002).

[73] Shihan de Jayasuriya and Richard Pankhurst, (eds.), *The African Diaspora in the Indian Ocean* (Trenton: Africa World Press, 2003).

[74] Hunwick and Powell, *The African Diaspora in the Mediterranean Lands of Islam*; and Jayasuriya and Pankhurst, *The African Diaspora in the Indian Ocean.*

[75] Jayasuriya and Pankhurst, *The African Diaspora in the Indian Ocean.*

[76] Jean Houbert, "Creolisation and decolonisation in the changing geopolitics of the Indian Ocean," in Jayasuriya and Pankhurst, (eds.), *The African Diaspora in the Indian Ocean* (Trenton, NJ: Africa World Press, 2003), 124.

Northwestern Africa – the Maghreb – is generally regarded as peripheral to Middle Eastern studies and extraneous to African studies. . . . Northwestern Africa (from Morocco to Libya), despite the area's close and enduring relationship with West Africa, has been excluded from the concerns of most Africanists.[77]

Zeleza returns to the original questions of who Africans are and what Africa is since they are necessary for a critical analysis of the African Diaspora. He ultimately views the continent as a history, a geography, and a constellation of places while asserting that his Africa is the Africa that consists of fifty-four countries and islands under the umbrella of the African Union (AU). It was a challenge to project this Africa backward in time to trace its specific history, but he found answers. History is often filtered from year to year and generation to generation through new and current lenses; as far as Africa is concerned, the perspective of the AU's predecessor, the Organization of African Unity (OAU), is particularly useful when compared to the racist African experience created through European imperialism.

Zeleza stresses that the Atlantic Diaspora differs from other continental diasporas, such as the West African Diasporas in North Africa and the East African Diasporas on the Indian Ocean islands. He suggests that the history of the African Diaspora has four divisions or categories based on their locations of dispersal.[78] These divisions include extra-continental diasporas, such as those in the Atlantic, Mediterranean, or Indian Oceans, and continental or intra-Africa diasporas.

The Atlantic Diaspora has well-detailed reviews and analyses that make its study easily accessible. In comparison, the study of intra-Africa diasporas is a challenge. Zeleza notes that constant, unstable migrations of Africans from one country to another over time are the source of the problem. The chronicles of nationalist historiography, of which the migration of the Bantu-speaking people is the most famous, emerged as an instance of the evolution of the African past. Zeleza explains that it would be insufficient to consider these movements as preludes to the emergence of diasporas within Africa, and he redirects his attention to African societies that are self-constituted or those made up of their host communities.

Zeleza categorized such societies into different diasporic systems based on their major reason for dispersal. The Somali and Fulani movements in the Sahelian zones of East and West Africa are identified as the pastoral diasporas, the remnants of the nineteenth century Yoruba wars are identified as refugee

---

[77] Hunwick and Powell, *The African Diaspora in the Mediterranean Lands of Islam*, xiii.

[78] The Trans-Saharan Diaspora, Indian Diaspora, Mediterranean Diaspora and the Atlantic Diaspora.

diasporas, the Nguni migration in South Africa is identified as the conquest diaspora, the East Africans on the Indian Ocean islands and West Africans in North Africa are identified as a slave diasporas, and the Dioula and Hausa shifts in West Africa are identified as trading diasporas. Apart from the trading and slave diasporas, these intracontinental diasporic systems have been uniquely studied without being qualified as "diasporas."[79]

Zeleza is not surprised that living diasporas have attracted more attention than others in recent comparative studies. He notes that the other diasporas existed and contributed immensely to the development of African Diaspora history in the twentieth century, which is why they should not be forgotten. Their effects, which served as the building blocks for national borders, should be recognized, and their diasporic identities should be reinforced whenever circuits of extra-continental migrations are being explored.

After he discusses the role of religion, especially Islam, in integrating slaves across the continent, Zeleza explains supplementary ideas in the works of other scholars. He ends with an additional explanation defining "the contours of the contemporary African diasporas."[80] Some faults have been recognized in "Rewriting the African Diaspora: Beyond the Black Atlantic," as the work fails to provide statistical evidence for most of its claims, and migration-related topics often demand numerical estimations to provide necessary context.

Conclusion

The diasporic movement of Africans is rich in history – Africa is a complex diasporic system and community with many unique migratory streams characterizing its evolution. These migratory streams develop distinct properties that are shaped by individual contexts. From pre-modern diasporic streams to their present-day counterparts, Africans have long been scattered across the surface of the earth. These movements have spurred a substantial amount of research and studies on the subject of African Diaspora history. Intellectuals and historians from within and beyond the continent have attempted to provide comprehensive accounts of the African Diaspora's history and its historical construction, but none has fully covered its global dimensions; these histories are grounded in and derived from a wide variety of geographic areas.

---

[79] Paul Tiyambe Zeleza, *A Modern Economic History of Africa, Vol 1: The Nineteenth Century* (Dakar: Codesria Book Series, 1993); Abner Cohen, "Cultural strategies in the organization of trading diasporas," in Claude Meillassoux, (ed.), *The Development of Indigenous Trade and Markets in West Africa* (London: Oxford University Press, 1971), 266–281; and Anthony G. Hopkins, *An Economic History of West Africa* (London: Longman, 1973).

[80] Zeleza, "Rewriting the African Diaspora," 54.

3 African Dispersals and the Concept of Overlapping Diaspora

Introduction

The concept of the African Diaspora has evolved to encompass not only the descendants of enslaved Africans but also all those of African descent who now live outside of Africa, either voluntarily or involuntarily. This includes people of African descent who have migrated to the Americas, Europe, and Asia in search of better economic opportunities, along with those who have been forced to migrate due to war, political instability, or persecution.[81] Although the African Diaspora is relatively broad as a concept, different groups of people encounter distinct diasporic experiences. One example is the transatlantic slave trade, which had a profound impact on the descendants of enslaved Africans; the experiences of slavery, segregation, and discrimination continue to shape their lives today.[82]

On the other hand, people of African descent who have more recently migrated to other parts of the world face different challenges and have different experiences. This is where the concept of an "overlapping diaspora" is useful to accommodate the fact that different groups of African descent have distinct diasporic experiences, but they also have overlapping experiences and connections.[83] African-Americans, Afro-Caribbeans, and Afro-Latinx groups all have unique histories, cultures, and identities, but they also share a common bond as people of African descent who live in the Americas. Their shared experiences can include racism and discrimination, and they have a collective interest in issues that relate to Africa and people of African descent around the world.[84]

Understanding the concept of an overlapping diaspora requires the acknowledgment that the African Diaspora is not limited to the Americas, Europe, and Asia; there are significant immigrant populations of African descent living in Africa itself, especially in countries such as South Africa, Kenya, and Senegal. These populations have distinct diasporic experiences, but they also have connections to other people of African descent elsewhere in the world. The idea of an overlapping diaspora is important for understanding the complexities of the African Diaspora, highlighting that people of African descent not only have distinct experiences and identities but also have shared experiences and

---

[81] Isidore Okpewho, Carole Boyce Davies, and Ali A. Mazrui, (eds.), *The African Diaspora: African Origins and New World Identities* (Bloomington: Indiana University Press, 2001).

[82] Rebecca Shumway, *The Fante and the Transatlantic Slave Trade* (Rochester: University of Rochester Press, 2014).

[83] Byfield, "Rethinking the African Diaspora," 1–9.

[84] Davies, (ed.), *Encyclopedia of the African Diaspora*.

connections. This understanding can build bridges between different groups of African descent and promote greater understanding and solidarity.

An Overview of the African Diaspora in the Context of Global Migrations

The African Diaspora has been shaped by a number of factors in the twentieth and twenty-first centuries, including decolonization, globalization, and changes in immigration policies. The end of colonial rule in Africa led to a new wave of migration as people sought greater economic opportunities in Europe and North America.[85] This migration was facilitated by globalization, which created new economic, social, and cultural links between countries. In many countries, changes in immigration policies made it easier for people to cross borders.

Today, the African Diaspora continues to have an impact on the lives and practices of those who descended from Africa. The transatlantic slave trade, with its forced migration of millions of Africans, was part of an ongoing phenomenon that spread African culture, language, and traditions throughout the world. Descendants of Africans have since made important contributions to cultures, economies, and politics in their adopted countries, reshaping national identities.

Black Movements in America,[86] by Cedric J. Robinson, explores the history and politics of Black social movements in the United States in the context of global migration and the African Diaspora. The book argues that Black US social movements have been shaped by complex interplays of race- and class-based oppression along with the wider historical and cultural forces of globalization. Robinson examines the role of Black social movements that shaped the struggles for civil rights and Black empowerment, identifying how these movements have been influenced by broader patterns of migration within the United States and globally. He argues that African-American experiences of slavery, segregation, and oppression are part of a larger pattern of racial exploitation and oppression that occurred throughout the world. In this context, Robinson explores the ways in which Black social movements resist and challenge these forces, examining how they have used the tools of migration, either voluntary or forced, to assert their rights and seek greater equality and justice. He also considers the ways in which these movements have interacted with other social movements, within the United States and internationally, to promote a more equitable and just world.

---

[85] Aristide R. Zolberg, "The next waves: Migration theory for a changing world," *International Migration Review* 23, 3 (1989): 403–430.

[86] Cedric J. Robinson, *Black Movements in America* (New York: Routledge, 2013).

However, *Black Movements in America* has some limits on its examination of the relationship between global migration and Black social movements. The book provides a detailed examination of the history and politics of Black social movements in the United States, but it only touches briefly on the experiences of African Diaspora communities in other parts of the world. The book was published in the early 1980s, and it primarily focuses on the history of Black US social movements up to that date – it cannot provide a comprehensive examination of more recent migration patterns and their impact on the African Diaspora. It also fails to consider intersectionality, despite the fact that it occupies itself with race and class, ignoring the nuanced ways in which gender, sexuality, and other identities intersect with and shape the experiences of African Diaspora communities.

The Black Atlantic, by Paul Gilroy, is another groundbreaking work exploring the experiences of the African Diaspora in the context of modernity and globalization. It argues that the forced migration of Africans to the Americas, as a result of the transatlantic slave trade, was a key factor in the development of modernity; the experiences of the African Diaspora shaped not only the cultures and societies of places in which they settled but also the wider forces of globalization. In this context, Gilroy argues that the African Diaspora has developed a unique form of cultural expression, which he calls the "Black Atlantic." This expression reflects the ways in which the African Diaspora has responded to the challenges and opportunities of globalization, and a sense of double consciousness or a dual awareness of African and European cultural influences characterizes it.

Gilroy draws on sources that include history, literature, music, and popular culture to illustrate the ways in which the African Diaspora has influenced and been influenced by globalization. He argues that the experiences of the African Diaspora, including slavery, segregation, and oppression, have profoundly affected the development of modernity and globalization; this impact is reflected in the cultural expressions of the "Black Atlantic." Gilroy's book is notable for its interdisciplinary approach, developing its analysis by drawing on insights from fields that include history, sociology, cultural studies, and literary studies. The book also provides a nuanced and insightful examination of the relationship between migration, identity, and culture, highlighting the ways in which the experiences of the African Diaspora have challenged and transformed dominant notions of race, identity, and cultural expression.

The Black Atlantic: Modernity and Double Consciousness is valuable and influential for scholars and students of the African Diaspora. It offers a comprehensive analysis of the African Diaspora's experiences and its impact on the development of modernity and globalization. This continues to be a relevant, important resource for those interested in understanding the relationship between migration, identity, and culture.

However, Gilroy's book has omitted other important aspects of the African Diaspora's experiences in the context of global migration, such as its economic and political dimensions. He provides an insightful analysis of the Black Atlantic's cultural expressions, but he does not explore the ways in which the transatlantic slave trade's forced migration of Africans impacted the economies of the Americas. The book also spends relatively little space discussing how African Diaspora communities have been involved in political struggles for independence, equality, and justice.

The Black Atlantic also lacks coverage of the African Diaspora's more recent experiences in the twentieth and twenty-first centuries. Gilroy provides a comprehensive analysis up to the late twentieth century, but he does not address the more recent experiences of African Diaspora communities in the context of globalization and the changing global political landscape.[87] The book fails to examine globalization's impact on the African Diaspora, which involved the flow of labor, ideas and goods, and the myriad of troubles and traumas faced by the enslaved and Blacks in general.[88]

Scholars and the Concept of Overlapping Diaspora

The concept of overlapping diaspora refers to the phenomenon where members of multiple diaspora communities interact and intersect in specific geographic locations. These interactions create unique cultural hybrids with a blending of traditions, customs, and identities. The concept recognizes that diaspora communities are neither isolated nor homogeneous but rather dynamic and constantly influencing each other.[89]

Flexible Citizenship: The Cultural Logics of Transnationality,[90] by Aihwa Ong, is a seminal work that explores the concept of overlapping diaspora and the cultural logic of transnationality. Ong examines the ways in which globalization and transnational migration have transformed the nature of citizenship and national belonging, arguing that the concept of flexible citizenship is a key feature of contemporary transnationality. Individuals are engaging in multiple, overlapping forms of belonging and affiliation that cross-national boundaries, which creates a hybrid cultural identity that is both local and global, often

---

[87] Peter Christoff and Robyn Eckersley, *Globalization and the Environment* (London: Rowman & Littlefield, 2013).

[88] Falola, *The African Diaspora*.

[89] Patterson and Kelley, "Unfinished migrations," 11–45.

[90] Aihwa Ong, *Flexible Citizenship: The Cultural Logics of Transnationality* (Durham: Duke University Press, 1999).

reflecting the intersection of multiple diaspora communities. Ong's analysis is based on her ethnographic research in Southeast Asia, where she has examined the experiences of transnational migrants and the cultural practices that emerged from their overlapping diaspora communities. Through her research, Ong shows how transnational migration instigated the creation of various cultural expressions and the reinforcement of existing ones; individuals draw on their multiple affiliations and identities to create unique cultural hybrids.

Flexible Citizenship has made a valuable contribution to the study of diaspora and transnationality, offering insights into the complexities of diaspora identity formation and globalization's impact on cultural practices and identities. However, like all works, it has its limitations. The book provides important insights into the concept of overlapping diaspora, but it is largely based on research conducted in Southeast Asia. It may not fully reflect the experiences of diaspora communities in other regions, and a more comparative approach would have provided a more nuanced understanding of the overlapping diaspora phenomenon.

Ong also emphasizes the cultural hybridity that emerges from overlapping diaspora communities, which can appear overly romanticized. Hybridity is not always positive or a desirable outcome of transnational migration, and the complexities of diaspora identity formation are often more nuanced than a mere blending of cultures. The book's theoretical framework oversimplifies the complex cultural, political, and economic processes that underlie transnational migration and diaspora identity formation – a more nuanced and interdisciplinary approach is required to evaluate the intricacies of these processes.

Nancy Foner's *From Ellis Island to JFK: New York's Two Great Waves of Immigration*[91] uses a sociological study of immigration to explore the formation of overlapping diaspora communities in New York City. The book focuses on two great waves of immigration during the late nineteenth and early twentieth centuries and the ways in which they shaped the city's social and cultural landscapes. Foner argues that the overlapping diaspora communities in New York City are a product of the city's history of immigration, asserting that they reflect the multiple, overlapping affiliations of immigrants and their descendants. She shows how these communities have both reinforced and challenged traditional notions of national and ethnic identity to create new cultural expressions and practices.

From Ellis Island to JFK draws on a rich array of sources, including census data, immigration records, and oral histories, to provide a detailed picture of the experiences of immigrants and their descendants in New York City. Foner's

---

[91] Nancy Foner, *From Ellis Island to JFK: New York's Two Great Waves of Immigration* (New Haven: Yale University Press, 2008).

work explores the ways in which immigration policies and the broader political and economic contexts have influenced the formation of these communities, making an important contribution to the study of immigration and overlapping diaspora communities.

However, the narrow geographic focus of Foner's book means that its findings may not be applicable to other regions or cities; a more comparative approach might have provided a more nuanced understanding of the phenomenon of overlapping diaspora. The book's focus on two great waves of immigration to New York City in the late nineteenth and early twentieth centuries also ignores more recent experiences among immigrants and diaspora communities. The lack of contemporary details concerning the formation of overlapping diaspora communities and the geographic focus on New York City may limit the work's applicability to other cities and regions.

James Clifford's *Routes: Travel and Translation in the Late Twentieth Century*[92] provides an open and vivid argument for the existence of overlapping diaspora. His work is a collection of essays exploring the relationships between travel, cultural exchange, and globalization. Clifford argues that diaspora communities are not fixed, bounded entities – instead, they are constantly in flux and subject to negotiation and redefinition. He contends that the cultural identities of diaspora communities are formed through a process of ongoing translation, performed by individuals and communities navigating the intersections of multiple cultural and national affiliations.

Clifford's perspective is particularly relevant to the concept of overlapping diaspora because it highlights the ways in which diaspora communities are not simply extensions of a single national or ethnic identity. Instead, they are complex, dynamic entities that reflect the multiple overlapping affiliations of their members. Clifford's focus on the fluidity and malleability of cultural identity has been widely influential in the field of diaspora and transnational studies, and it has shifted the focus from viewing diaspora communities as bounded entities to a more nuanced understanding of the ways in which they are constantly in flux and subject to ongoing negotiation and redefinition. These insights into the relationships between travel, cultural exchange, and globalization, along with the focus on the fluidity and malleability of cultural identity, continue to shape the way that scholars and others understand the experiences of overlapping diaspora communities. Clifford's book is an important contribution to the field of diaspora and transnational studies, and it continues to be widely read and highly regarded.

---

[92] James Clifford, *Routes: Travel and Translation in the Late Twentieth Century* (Cambridge, MA: Harvard University Press, 1997).

However, there are areas within the concept of overlapping diaspora that remain unexamined in *Routes*. The book does not address how political and economic factors, such as immigration policies, labor market dynamics, and the impact of globalization, shape the experiences of overlapping diaspora communities.[93] It also provides superficial coverage of the ways in which overlapping diaspora communities are shaped by power dynamics and social inequalities that include racism, sexism, and colonialism.[94] These are important areas of inquiry for understanding the experiences of overlapping diaspora communities. It is noteworthy that the book is not an exhaustive treatment of the concept of overlapping diaspora – it is a collection of essays that explore specific aspects of travel, cultural exchange, and globalization. Overall, Clifford's work remains an important contribution to the field of diaspora and transnational studies that continues to influence how scholars and others understand the experiences of overlapping diaspora communities.[95]

Paul Gilroy's *The Black Atlantic* is widely regarded as one of the most important books on the subject of overlapping diasporas. Gilroy argues that the experiences of African Diaspora communities in the Americas, Europe, and Africa cannot be understood as isolated, disconnected phenomena. Instead, they must be seen as part of a larger, interconnected "Black Atlantic" world. This world is characterized by a complex interplay of cultural exchange, political resistance, and economic exploitation, and the cultural identities of Black diaspora communities are shaped by these ongoing processes. He also argues that the experiences of Black diaspora communities are characterized by a "double consciousness" where individuals and communities navigate the intersections of multiple cultural and national affiliations to negotiate the competing demands of different cultural and political identities. Gilroy's insights into the Black Atlantic world and his focus on the complex interplay of cultural exchange, political resistance, and economic exploitation have shaped public understanding of the experiences of overlapping diaspora communities in the Americas, Europe, and Africa.

The Black Atlantic also has its limitations. Although Gilroy's focus on the Black Atlantic world is innovative and influential, his framework is generally limited to the experiences of African Diaspora communities in the Americas, Europe, and Africa. This narrow focus may exclude the complex experiences of

---

[93] Giles Mohan and Alfred B. Zack-Williams, "Globalisation from below: Conceptualising the role of the African Diasporas in Africa's development," *Review of African Political Economy* 29, 92 (2002): 211–236.

[94] Vivek Bald, "Overlapping diasporas, multiracial lives: South Asian Muslims in US communities of color, 1880–1950," *Souls* 8, 4 (2006): 3–18.

[95] Earl Lewis, "To turn as on a pivot: Writing African Americans into a history of overlapping diasporas," *The American Historical Review* 100, 3 (1995): 765–787.

overlapping diaspora communities that exist in other regions of the world. And despite its focus on the Black Atlantic world, Gilroy's book is criticized for adopting a Eurocentric perspective that privileges the experiences of African Diaspora communities in Europe over those in the Americas and Africa.

Some critics have accused Gilroy of essentializing the experiences of Black diaspora communities, suggesting that his monolithic view of these groups obscures their diverse and complex experiences individually and collectively. Although Gilroy addresses the ways in which power dynamics shape the experiences of Black diaspora communities, he neither provides a nuanced analysis of these forces nor fully explores the ways in which different systems of oppression intersect and interact. These details do not diminish the significance of Gilroy's contributions to the field of diaspora and transnational studies – instead, they highlight ways in which his framework can be expanded or refined.

Understanding the Cases of Overlapping Diaspora in the African Diaspora

The overlapping diaspora concept highlights the presence of multiple diaspora communities within a single host country or region, recognizing the ways in which these communities influence and interact with each other. In the African Diaspora, this phenomenon can be observed in several countries where multiple diaspora communities coexist and contribute to local cultural and economic development. One of the most notable examples of overlapping diaspora is the African Diaspora in Europe,[96] which encompasses a significant number of African communities that have relocated to various countries, such as the UK and Germany. These communities bring a rich cultural heritage that includes music, dance, cuisine, and religious beliefs that have contributed to the cultural diversity of their host countries. The African Diaspora in Europe has significantly shaped the political and social evolution of host countries by advocating for the rights and interests of African communities while promoting African culture and heritage.[97]

Another example of an overlapping diaspora is the Indian diaspora in Africa.[98] Communities of Indians living in African countries, including Kenya, Tanzania, and South Africa, have established businesses that contribute to their local economies. The Indian Diaspora has also established cultural and

---

[96] Darlene Clark Hine, Trica Danielle Keaton, and Stephen Small, (eds.), *Black Europe and the African Diaspora* (Champaign: University of Illinois Press, 2009).

[97] John A. Arthur, *The African Diaspora in the United States and Europe: The Ghanaian Experience* (London: Routledge, 2016).

[98] Ajay Dubey, (ed.), *Indian Diaspora in Africa: A Comparative Perspective* (New Delhi: Organisation for Diaspora Initiatives, African Studies Association of India & MD Publications, 2010).

religious connections between India and Africa through the promotion of Hinduism, Buddhism, and other Indian religious and cultural traditions.[99] The Indian Diaspora's establishment of trade and investment connections between India and Africa has played a significant role in shaping the economic landscape of their host countries.[100]

A growing population of Chinese immigrants in countries such as Nigeria, South Africa, and Egypt constitutes a Chinese Diaspora in Africa. These individuals have made investments in infrastructure and industry that have established cultural and economic ties between China and Africa. The Chinese Diaspora has shaped political developments in host countries by advocating for the interests of Chinese communities and promoting Chinese culture and heritage.

The Lebanese Diaspora in Africa is yet another example of an overlapping diaspora. Significant populations of Lebanese descent have settled in countries that include Senegal, Ghana, and Ivory Coast, where they have established businesses and contributed to the local economy.[101] The Lebanese Diaspora has created cultural and religious connections between Lebanon and Africa through the promotion of Lebanese cuisine, music, and other cultural traditions. The Lebanese diaspora has also influenced economic developments in host countries by establishing trade and investment connections between Lebanon and Africa.[102]

In exploring this subject matter, Ira Bashkow's *The Meaning of Whitemen: Race and Modernity in the Orokaiva Cultural World*[103] is a groundbreaking work in the field of anthropology; it explores the complex and dynamic experiences of the Orokaiva people in Papua New Guinea.[104] The book examines how cultural identities are shaped by the overlapping influences of colonialism, Christianity, and globalization, offering insights into the ongoing negotiation and transformation of cultural practices and beliefs in the contemporary world.

---

[99] Amit Kumar Jain, Upendra Nabh Tripathi, and Vinita Katiyar, "An overview on Indian Diaspora in Africa," *Educational Quest-An International Journal of Education and Applied Social Sciences* 8, 1 (2017): 17–22.

[100] Ajay K. Dubey, "India and experience of Indian Diaspora in Africa," *Africa Quarterly* 40, 2 (2000): 69–92.

[101] Andrew Arsan, *Interlopers of Empire: The Lebanese Diaspora in Colonial French West Africa* (Oxford: Oxford University Press, 2014).

[102] Emmanuel K. Akyeampong, "Race, identity and citizenship in Black Africa: The case of the Lebanese in Ghana," *Africa* 76, 3 (2006): 297–323.

[103] Ira Bashkow, *The Meaning of Whitemen: Race and Modernity in the Orokaiva Cultural World* (Chicago: University of Chicago Press, 2017).

[104] Francis Edgar Williams and Hubert Murray, *Orokaiva Society, with an Introduction by Sir Hubert Murray* (London: Oxford University Press, 1930).

Bashkow's book provides a detailed and nuanced ethnographic analysis of the Orokaiva people based on extensive fieldwork and interviews that provide a rich and nuanced understanding of the Orokaiva cultural world, detailing their beliefs, practices, and experiences. Bashkow delivers a rich historical context that traces the Orokaiva culture's interactions with colonialism, Christianity, and globalization, along with its evolution over time.[105] The book also examines the intersection of race, power, and cultural identity. Bashkow provides a sophisticated analysis of these different factors interacting and shaping cultural identities, particularly in the context of colonialism and globalization. He argues that the Orokaiva's experiences of colonialism and globalization have been shaped by their race and by the ways in which outsiders perceive them –these experiences have had a profound impact on the evolution of the Orokaiva cultural identity.

The Meaning of Whitemen makes valuable contributions to the studies of cultural identity and overlapping diaspora, but it focuses specifically on the Orokaiva people in Papua New Guinea and their experiences with colonialism, Christianity, and globalization. This limits the book's applicability to other overlapping diaspora cases. In merely providing an analysis of the Orokaiva situation, the book does not offer comparisons with other overlapping diasporas in the Pacific region or elsewhere, which could have provided additional insights into the broader phenomenon. Bashkow's analysis is also based on ethnographic research, which is limited by the perspectives and experiences of his interviewees, and it may not capture the full diversity of experiences and perspectives within the Orokaiva community. Additionally, the book's argument that colonialism, Christianity, and globalization have dominantly shaped the Orokaiva cultural identity may be an oversimplification of these complex, multifaceted processes.

Conclusion

The African Diaspora is a story of human resilience, endurance, and creativity. Despite centuries of slavery, oppression, and discrimination, people of African descent have not only survived but also thrived in their new homes. They have created vibrant, dynamic communities that add value to the cultures of places where they have lived.

The overlapping diaspora concept highlights the complex, layered identities maintained by people of African descent, and it underscores the importance of recognizing and valuing the diversity of these experiences and perspectives. In an increasingly interconnected world, it is more important than ever to understand and appreciate the complexities of the African Diaspora. The recognition of the

---

[105] André Iteanu, "The concept of the person and the ritual system: An Orokaiva view," *Man* 25, 1 (1990): 35–53.

overlapping connections existing between different diaspora communities can foster greater understanding, respect, and collaboration among people of African descent around the world. By celebrating the rich cultural heritage and contributions of the African Diaspora, we can create a more inclusive and equitable world for all people, regardless of their background.

4 Rethinking the African Diaspora

Introduction

Africa has a rich, complex history that is integral to the history of humanity itself. Today's modern world exists because of Africa; it has been involved in everything from enslavement to urbanization, industrialization, and globalization in the ongoing evolution of a globally connected world.

Africa's people, and those who are descended from them, have a history that is not isolated to a specific nation or region. Instead, their story intertwines with associations and interconnections between people across the continents of the world, including Europe, the Americas, and Asia. This history includes the collective migrations of people – neither separate nor isolated – who leave and return to the continent through fluid pathways such as the Indian Ocean, the Mediterranean Sea, and the Atlantic Ocean.[106] Africans have continuously been on the move for many centuries, migrating and voyaging from one place to another, either voluntarily or by force. These developments have metamorphosed into today's African Diaspora.

To understand the African Diaspora, it is necessary to acknowledge Africa and its people; these concepts are integral to a critical analysis of the African Diaspora. Africa has been described as an imagined place, a geography, a historical settlement, a history and a story, and a constellation of settlements.[107] It comprises fifty-four countries that are scattered across the horizons and highways of the world, and its people have settled in every part of the globe. The term "Africans" collectively refers to all people of African descent whose origins, ways of life, cultures, and existences can be traced to Africa. They are not bounded or limited by location – for every African, a self-consciousness and an awareness of being seen as an African is an indispensable factor. This is what defines them as Africans and unites them as one, as they continue building their experiences.

As noted already (see p. 14), the concept of the African Diaspora emerged relatively recently, around the 1950s and 1960s. The complexity surrounding

---

[106] Patrick Manning, *The African Diaspora: A History through Culture* (New York: Columbia University Press, 2010).

[107] Paul Zeleza, "Africa: The changing meanings of 'African' culture and identity," in Elisabeth Abiri and Håkan Thörn, (eds.), *Horizons: Perspectives on a Global Africa* (Lund: Studentlitteratur, 2005), 31–72.

the meaning and fundamental qualities of the word diaspora make it difficult to transcend its discursive politics. One scholar's frustration with the process led him to state that the term "diaspora" has "imposed a US and English language centered model of black identity on the complex experiences of populations of African descent."[108] Instead, people of African descent have been more commonly mobilized through concepts such as Pan-Africanism.

To retain its analytical specificity and relevance in a comparative study, the term "diaspora" must be conceived in a way that is bounded but not restrictively narrow. Diaspora, or a diasporic identity as described by Zeleza, refers to "a form of group consciousness constituted historically through expressive culture, politics, thought and tradition, in which experiential and representational resources are mobilized from the imaginaries of both the old and the new worlds."[109] Zeleza explains that diasporas "are complex social and cultural communities created out of real and imagined genealogies and geographies (cultural, racial, ethnic, national, continental, transnational) of belonging, displacement, and recreation, constructed and conceived at multiple temporal and spatial scales, at different moments and distances from the putative homeland."[110]

The task of defining an African Diaspora has been so complex that several scholars have resorted to ethnocentric contexts, using experiences that are specific to individual societies and communities as universal representations of an African Diaspora. Other scholars have encountered linguistic challenges in engaging with the massive volume of discourse, literature, and languages that prevent them from attempting a global overview of the African Diaspora. Instead, they have limited their efforts to the Americas alone. The conceptualization of an African Diaspora remains debated by many scholars.

In George Shepperson's "African Diaspora: Concept and Context,"[111] included in *Global Dimensions of the African Diaspora*,[112] Shepperson argues that no major intellectual work – from Edward W. Blyden to W.E.B. Du Bois – touches on the topic while using the term African Diaspora. Evidently, "it originated in the English-speaking world, where it received most of its development to date." Shepperson argues that the study of the African diaspora not only encourages a comparative approach, but also has much to gain when examined from the perspectives of other non-English languages, such as those

---

[108] Brent Hayes Edwards, "'Unfinished migrations': Commentary and response," *African Studies Review* 43, 1 (2000): 47.

[109] Zeleza, "Rewriting the African Diaspora," 41.

[110] Zeleza, "Rewriting the African Diaspora," 41–42.

[111] George Shepperson, "African Diaspora: Concept and context," in Joseph E. Harris, (ed.), *Global Dimensions of the African Diaspora* 2nd ed., (Washington, D.C.: Howard University Press, 1993) 41–49.

[112] Harris, *Global Dimensions of the African Diaspora*.

from Europe, Asia, Africa, and those that have resulted from the exchanges between African and non-African cultures.[113]

The term "African Diaspora" has been described as "all global communities descended from the historic migrations of peoples from Africa since the fifteenth century which delineates it from the prehistoric out-of-Africa migrations that led to the peopling of the world."[114] This diaspora has been perceived from different perspectives, including that of the transatlantic slave trade, which remains an influential historical event for the African Diaspora.[115] Many scholars have observed the importance of geography, racism, colonialism, slavery, and Blackness in continuing the slave trade and ultimately conceptualizing the Black Diaspora, which is a term that is often used interchangeably with African Diaspora.[116]

Due to growing interest in the field, many studies and research works have emerged to address the African Diaspora, created by authors and writers, including African historians and scholars. Their foreign counterparts have also launched studies into the historical evolution of the African Diaspora.

A critical review of major books, journals, and literature – from the traditional narrative to alternative perspectives on the subject and discussions of the African Diaspora's role in shaping global history and culture – can bridge the wide gaps in public understanding of the subject, exposing its integral parts and areas of discussion yet to be fully analyzed.

Rethinking the Traditional Narrative of the African Diaspora

The conventional account of the African Diaspora focuses on the historical significance of the transatlantic slave trade and its lasting effects. This narrative traces back to the sixteenth century and extends until the nineteenth century. This narrative delves into the profound and distressing experiences of countless Africans who were forcefully uprooted from their homes, predominantly from West and Central Africa, and subjected to the unspeakable horrors of the slave trade. This account provides a detailed portrayal of the magnitude and cruelty of this trade, which remains one of the most significant forced migrations in the annals of humanity. Over twelve million individuals were transported across the Atlantic Ocean to the Americas and the Caribbean, leaving an indelible mark on history.

---

[113] Shepperson, "African Diaspora," 44.

[114] Charles N. Rotimi, Fasil Tekola-Ayele, Jennifer L Baker, and Daniel Shriner, "The African Diaspora: History, adaptation and health," *Current Opinion in Genetics & Development* 41 (2016): 77.

[115] David Eltis, "The US transatlantic slave trade, 1644–1867: An assessment," *Civil War History* 54, 4 (2008): 347–378.

[116] Segal, *The Black Diaspora.*

Central to this narrative is the Middle Passage, a notorious and treacherous voyage across the Atlantic, where enslaved Africans faced deplorable conditions characterized by overcrowding, widespread disease, and unrelenting mistreatment. The narrative progresses as they reached the New World, where they were compelled to endure a grueling existence of strenuous work, primarily in plantation agriculture, enduring ceaseless subjugation and exploitation. In the face of these challenging circumstances, the story beautifully portrays the strength and determination of African people. It emphasizes the remarkable ability of enslaved Africans to preserve and modify aspects of their vibrant and varied cultural heritage, resulting in the emergence of unique, blended cultures in the Americas. This cultural fusion is apparent in various aspects of life, from the evolution of Creole languages and religious practices to unique musical and culinary traditions. The narrative also highlights the different ways in which enslaved Africans resisted their captors, showcasing their unwavering determination for freedom and self-respect.

The narrative of the African Diaspora also encompasses the gradual elimination of both the slave trade and slavery itself worldwide. It explores the ongoing challenges for civil rights, acknowledgment, and equality experienced by liberated Africans and their offspring, as well as the lasting impacts of slavery, including racial bias and socio-economic inequalities. The story concludes with the establishment of diaspora communities, where the offspring of enslaved Africans have crafted fresh identities by blending African, European, and indigenous American influences, resulting in distinct cultural identities.

This narrative has played a crucial role in shedding light on the harrowing experiences of millions of Africans who were forcibly displaced and transported to the Americas, enduring indescribable challenges. It provides a vivid portrayal of the grueling voyage across the Atlantic, commonly referred to as the Middle Passage, and the stark truths of existence under enslavement. In addition, it highlights the strength of African cultures and the development of diverse, blended identities in the diaspora. Nevertheless, this conventional account, though fundamental, is now regarded as somewhat limited in the present era of a more interconnected and globalized comprehension of history and identity. A significant drawback is the excessive focus on the transatlantic slave trade, which, although important, does not fully encompass the African Diaspora's defining experiences. Often, the emphasis on certain aspects overlooks African societies' fascinating and intricate pre-colonial histories. These histories were incredibly dynamic and multifaceted, existing independently of the subsequent European influence and the slave trade.

In addition, the conventional narrative may at times fail to acknowledge the autonomy and influence of African individuals and societies, often depicting them primarily as victims. This perspective overlooks the extensive and dynamic contributions made by Africans, who actively resisted and skillfully navigated the challenges posed by the slave trade and colonial rule. Furthermore, it often oversimplifies the richness and complexity of the African Diaspora, failing to fully encompass the diverse experiences and identities found among different African ethnic groups and regions.

Another important aspect to consider is the narrative's emphasis on forced migration, sometimes overlooking other expansions of the African Diaspora, such as voluntary migrations for trade, education, or labor. These historical and contemporary movements have had a profound impact on shaping the global African experience. They remain highly relevant today, characterized by complex and multifaceted migration patterns. The ever-changing nature of diaspora identities in the context of modern issues such as globalization, transnationalism, and the digital age also demands a more comprehensive and all-encompassing narrative. Although essential as a foundation, the conventional framework may not completely capture these modern dimensions and the ever-evolving nature of diasporic identities in the present day.

The African Diaspora encompasses geographic regions and the dispersal of Africans and their descendants in the earliest centuries. There has been disagreement over whether the word "dispersal" appropriately describes the African Diaspora's history; Kelley and Patterson have specifically noted that a dispersal is not the same as a diaspora.[117] These scholars insist that the emergence of a diaspora largely depends on a diasporic identity that connects the parts of such diasporic systems with their original territories. The development of such an identity is not always a natural occurrence. The African Diaspora only exists due to its historical, cultural, and social construction, reconstruction, and recreation, which becomes evident when critically examining the diasporic identities of African descendants in the Americas, the Arabian Peninsula, the Indian subcontinent, along with other parts of the world.

Among the African Diaspora's many historical narratives, Colin Palmer's account enjoys substantial popularity due to its distinctly detailed accounts of when and where African diasporic movements began. In "Defining and Studying the Modern African Diaspora," Palmer identified five major diasporic streams that contributed to the current concept of the African Diaspora.[118] In words and practice, the African Diaspora is not a single diasporic movement – it stems from myriads of movements and migrations that date back 100,000

---

[117] Patterson and Kelly, "Unfinished migrations," 11–45.
[118] Davies, (ed.), *Encyclopedia of the African Diaspora*.

years.[119] Palmer asserts that the movement of African descendants within and beyond the continent during this period characterized the first diasporic stream.

Palmer argues that these earliest diasporic movements must be included in the traditional African Diaspora narrative, although some scholars disagree. The controversy stems from the dissimilarities between early African migration patterns and subsequent or contemporary migrations, especially regarding their nature and characteristics. However, Palmer maintains that any research on the migration and settlement of African descendants can only be complete if it recognizes the earliest movements. He has opened the issue for debate and discussion among scholars.[120]

The second diasporic stream only involved the Bantu-speaking people, a population of Africans that occupy territory in the current-day nations of Cameron and Nigeria. These intracontinental and intercontinental migrations occurred around 3,000 B.C.E.[121] – Africans migrated to the Indian Ocean and other regions and countries on the African continent.

The third diasporic stream emerged around the fifth century B.C.E.[122] Unlike its predecessors, Palmer describes this movement as a trading diaspora. African soldiers, traders, slavers, slaves, and merchants moved from the African continent to some parts of Asia, the Middle East, and Europe. The migratory pace of this third diasporic stream was largely uneven, with varied textures and structures that lasted for an indefinite number of years. The Muslim-oriented and facilitated slave trade, which roiled the seventh century and forcefully migrated many Africans to the Middle East and the Mediterranean, is not conceived as a new diasporic movement; it is an offshoot of the third diasporic movement that exhibited an unprecedented scope and energy.[123]

The evolution and ongoing existence of the third diasporic stream established a wide variety of African communities in parts of Italy, Spain, Portugal, and other European nations, along with groups in India, Middle Eastern countries, and Asia. The creation of these African communities took place long before Christopher Columbus launched his expeditions and voyages across the Atlantic.[124] Palmer references Frank Snowden's works on Africa and African descendants in the classical period[125] to emphasize this stream's relevance to

---

[119] Zeleza, "Rewriting the African Diaspora," 35–68.

[120] Chris Stringer and Robin McKie, *African Exodus: The Origins of Modern Humanity* (London: Macmillan, 1998).

[121] Palmer, "Defining and studying the modern African Diaspora," 27–32.

[122] Palmer, "Social Movements in the African Diaspora during the Twentieth Century."

[123] Palmer, "The African diaspora," 56–59.

[124] Christopher Stringer and Robin McKie, *African Exodus: The Origins of Modern Humanity* (New York: Henry Holt, 1996).

[125] Snowden Jr., *Blacks in Antiquity*.

and indispensability for the narrative of the African Diaspora. He points out that Snowden has found it impossible to ascertain the exact number of Ethiopians – a term that was previously used to refer to Africans in general – involved in commercial, diplomatic, and military activities during the Greco–Roman era.

Palmer conceptualizes the first three diasporic streams as the pre-modern African Diaspora, and the fourth and fifth diasporic streams are described as the modern African Diaspora. He acknowledges that other diasporic movements have taken place after the fifth diasporic stream and that they are integral parts of the modern African Diaspora, but the fourth diasporic stream is the most widely studied. This fourth stream accounts for the transatlantic slave trade, which removed 200,000 Africans from their homeland and exported them to different European countries for commercial purposes. The same slave trade also resettled approximately twelve million Africans at destinations in the Americas. This abhorrent activity composed the majority of trade in the fifteenth century, and it has continued to attract the attention of scholars and historians researching and studying its origin, scope, and relevance to the study of the African Diaspora. The fifth diasporic stream emerged later, in the nineteenth century. This category includes recent diasporic movements and the post-transatlantic migrations of African descendants. Recent diasporic movements are characterized by the constant movement of Africans and their settlement in various foreign communities.

Palmer identifies other significant African migrations, apart from these diasporic streams, that must be included in a complete narrative of the African Diaspora. The nature, scope, and timing of these complementary diasporic streams must be analyzed distinctly to avoid conflating them with each other. They include the migration of Africans from the eastern part of the African continent to Asia and the Middle East shortly after the transatlantic slave trade ended. A diasporic movement of Africans between 2,500 B.C.E and 2,300 B.C.E also occurred due to climate change in the Sahara. These primary and complementary diasporic movements are carefully examined and illustrated by Palmer to form the essential foundation of the African Diaspora's traditional narrative.

Palmer's work is detailed and thorough, but it fails to illustrate how each of these diasporic streams affected the continent of Africa and its people. These movements shaped the mental, physical, and social perspectives of their participants, and their effects should be included in the narrative of the African Diaspora. Although Palmer provides important details that include dates and locations, this additional information could be considered as a supplement. Africans and people of African descent venerate the experiences of their predecessors and ancestors, which is why their inclusion would have elevated Palmer's analysis.

"Defining and Studying the Modern African Diaspora" contributes to the historical evolution of the African Diaspora, covering a period that ranges from the fifth century to the late nineteenth century, but the work is relatively limited in some respects. Its title includes the word "modern," but it fails to expound on the contemporary issues that surround the African Diaspora, including regional underdevelopment due to the brain drain.[126] Most of the diasporic streams that Palmer discusses, especially the fourth stream, conveniently illustrate this phenomenon of a brain drain; a proper discussion of the issue could have examined how modern Africa remains challenged by ongoing shortages of skilled labor.

Palmer's work is also light on details regarding the motivations that drove migrations outside of the third and fourth diasporic streams. He explains that the third and fourth diasporic streams were mainly orchestrated for commercial and industrial purposes, but similar motives are not provided for the others. Readers are left wondering whether these diasporic streams were motivated by political, social, cultural, or even economic factors.

Rethinking the African Diaspora: Alternative Perspectives

On May 13, 1888, Africans and other victims of slavery were officially freed from their shackles of oppression and servitude as Brazil became the last country to abolish slavery.[127] Although slavery was ceased, the official declaration was not completely effective; slavery in the modern world has not been completely eradicated. Most of the people forcibly moved or migrated from their home territories to other parts of the world were African, and these travels took them to the Americas, the Middle East, Asia, and Europe.[128] These migrations constitute the African Diaspora, which can be seen as many branches growing outward from the tree of Africa.

The pressing need to examine the relationship between the tree and its branches, or the continent and its diasporic streams, along with the interconnection between branches and streams themselves, is contemporaneously and historically important. Africa's enslavement was the main outcome of the transatlantic slave trade. The enslaved, and later the voluntary immigrants

---

[126] A. E. Nunn and Sophia Price, "The 'brain drain': Academic and skilled migration to the UK and its impacts on Africa." Report to the AUT and NATFHE. 2005.

[127] George Shepperson, "The African abroad or the African Diaspora," *African Forum* 2, 1 (1966): 76–93.

[128] Blaine Hudson, "The African Diaspora and the Black Atlantic: An African American perspective," *Negro History Bulletin* 60, 4 (1997): 7–14.

were able to bring their cultures, bodies, and ways of life to new destinations, particularly in the Americas.[129] Ongoing inquiry asks what became of these bodies and cultural heritages – do they remember Africa? And if so, what unique attributes can they recall? Research seeks to identify what was changed, maintained, or lost when these migrants were prevented from passing their history on to the next generation. Inquiries also study whether there has been a partial or complete loss of connection to African culture. These concerns and others have birthed diverse perspectives on the African Diaspora.

African-American perspectives on the African Diaspora are useful for unraveling the subject's political, cultural, and historical implications; Blaine Hudson's "The African Diaspora and the Black Atlantic: An African American Perspective," makes significant contributions to these perspectives. After a comprehensive description of the African Diaspora's history and evolution, Hudson recounts how Africans who had been captured as slaves, especially during the transatlantic slave trade, were the driving force behind industrial advancements in the United States and Europe.

Hudson explains that this extraction, for the benefit of the Americas, caused intense disruptions in African societies and established the African Diaspora as a system of related yet distinct experiences. The distinctions among these experiences are reflected through similar themes, such as a common condition, common origins, and common host nations or communities.[130] Hudson asserts that when examining the African Diaspora through modern lenses, it can be seen to result in a kind of slavery that metamorphoses into a complete loss of civil and political freedom. He stresses that although financial and economic forces principally drove the majority of diasporic movements among Africans and their descendants, the cultural implications must be borne by Black and White individuals collectively.[131] Enslaved Africans were driven by a motive to survive, while interests in the Americas were solely concerned with creating new sources of revenue.

Although Africans found it culturally difficult to adapt to their new surroundings, their American and European counterparts benefitted from barriers and conditions that adversely affected people of African descent.[132] Everyone endured the struggles to adapt – even Europeans who had migrated to the

---

[129] Vincent B. Thompson, *The Making of the African Diaspora in the Americas 1441–1900* (New York: Longman, 1987), 1–4.

[130] John H. Franklin and Alfred A. Moss, *From Slavery to Freedom: A History of African Americans* (New York: McGraw-Hill, 1984), 33–35.

[131] Sterling Stuckey, *Slave Culture: Nationalist Theory and the Foundations of Black America* (New York: Oxford University, 1987).

[132] Herbert S. Klein, *African Slavery in Latin America and the Caribbean* (New York: Oxford University, 1986), 10–12.

Americas underwent great cultural transformations triggered by their new societies. Regardless of how successfully these individuals struggled to retain aspects of their European identities, their new and radically distinct environments led successive descendants to claim citizenship in their place of birth rather than their country of origin.[133]

Not only did people of African descent in the Americas have to endure the same transformational forces as their European counterparts, but they also had their lives and existences controlled by white owners. Hudson explains that "their existential universe and the minute details of their everyday lives were influenced and regulated by the cultural and institutional expressions of the ideology of white racial supremacy."[134] However, he also asserts that Blacks were not passive while suffering under this oppression. Africans were propelled by a desire to survive, be free, and retain their human nature, which proved to be more enduring motives than the White agenda of maintaining unchallenged control and exploitation. Although Africans lacked the influence and power of their oppressors, they were not entirely vulnerable or without cultural tools and resources.

Despite the fact that Africans originated from diverse societies before their enslavement and transport to the Americas, they were largely united by common cultural, religious, and linguistic attributes.[135] As they improved their relationships with one another, they simultaneously built a common body of cultural practices, values, and views. However, it was difficult to adapt these cultural practices to the Americas because Whites vilified such traditions as archaic, unchristian, and dangerous. Hudson's work discusses the servitude and cultural assimilations under which people of African descent suffered.

Hudson spends several pages recounting the bitter trials that Africans endured, but these experiences are limited to those from Europe and the Americas. His work fails to explore the experiences of Africans in the Mediterranean, the Indian Ocean, the Middle East, and Asia. Africans have migrated to a wide range of locations, and it would be useful to describe the African diasporic experiences in these areas. The book is also limited by covering a single diasporic movement: the transatlantic slave trade. This narrow focus omits the other diasporic streams identified by Palmer, although it

---

[133] Hilary H. Beckles, *White Servitude and Black Slavery in Barbados 1627–1715* (Knoxville: University of Tennessee, 1989).

[134] Alan G. Cobley and Alvin Thompson, (eds.), *The African-Caribbean Connection: Historical and Cultural Perspectives* (Barbados: University of the West Indies, 1990), 1–27.

[135] Sterling Stuckey, *Going through the Storm: The Influence of African American Art in History* (Oxford: Oxford University, 1994).

provides a thorough perspective on the African Diaspora from an African-American point of view.

St. Clair Drake's "The Black Diaspora in Pan-African Perspective"[136] offers another perspective on the African Diaspora while sharing similarities with Hudson's "The African Diaspora and the Black Atlantic." Drake's central idea revolves around the highly popularized African diasporic movements that occurred from 1,500 A.D to 1,890 A.D.[137] Drake asserts that ten million people of African descent migrated to Western communities during this period.

Drake examines the experiences of Africans who were enslaved by Europeans and made to work in various venues that included plantations, yeoman farms, mines, and maritime facilities. They were consistently placed in subordinate roles during production processes, regardless of specific times or places.[138] Institutionalized racial discrimination made their situation worse – for more than 300 years, slaves were racially abused, and free individuals experienced discrimination. Their work was categorized as "free" labor under socially stratified systems described as caste systems and color–class systems.[139] These systems trapped Africans at society's lowest level, denying them access to financial resources and economic opportunities.[140] The phenomenon of "false consciousness" also blinded Africans to the possibility of taking active steps toward their emancipation.

Drake's summary asserts that 115 years after the abolition of slavery, "the black community in the United States represented the largest, most compact, and best-organized group in the hemisphere that considered itself 'black' – composed of some 24,000,000 individuals . . . . .yet, its leadership potential in Pan-African affairs is complicated by the fact that it is enclaved within the territory of a large white superpower."[141]

Drake's perspective on the African Diaspora, like Hudson's, focuses mainly on the transatlantic slave trade, and it omits views and ideas connected to the migration of Africans to other parts of the world. His work focuses on a single diasporic stream and the economic exploitation of Africans in Europe and the Americas; it neglects broader political and cultural implications.

---

[136] St. Clair Drake, "The Black Diaspora in Pan-African perspective," *The Black Scholar* 7, 1 (1975): 2–13.

[137] Philip D. Curtin, "The Slave trade and the Atlantic basin: Intercontinental perspectives," in Nathan I. Huggins, Martin Kilson, and Daniel M. Fox, (eds.), *Key Issues in the Afro-American Experience*, Vol. I, (Brace Jovanovich: Harcourt, 1971), 74–93.

[138] Carl N. Degler, *Neither Black Nor White: Slavery and Race Relations in Brazil and the United States* (New York: Collier, 1971).

[139] Allison Davis, Burleigh Gardner, and Mary Gardner, *Deep South: A Social Anthropological Study of Caste and Class* (Chicago: University of Chicago Press, 1941).

[140] Davis, Gardner, and Gardner, *Deep South*.

[141] Drake, "The Black Diaspora in Pan-African perspective," 2.

Reexamining the Role of the African Diaspora in Shaping Global History and Culture

Diasporas, and the African Diaspora in particular, have emerged as a prominent feature of global policy development.[142] From the continent of Africa to elsewhere in the world, the African Diaspora has been a driving force behind profound developments in global history and culture. The frequent portrayal of migrations – and diasporas above all – as essential historical events have contributed to conflict resolution and social reconstruction that improves not only coexistence among people from different continental and national backgrounds but also developmental interventions in a rapidly evolving world.

Many diasporas, including the Jewish Diaspora and its African counterpart, have collectively been embraced for their potential to promote " . . . ideal forms of politics that are not only essentially non-threatening to dominant neoliberal orders but which also bear little resemblance to the ways in which politics actually work in developing countries."[143] The influence of diasporic movements that involve people of African descent can be seen reflected in historical and geographical contexts.

The African Diaspora's impact has not been limited to any specific geographic setting; it has been an all-inclusive process that cuts across a wide variety of countries, regions, and continents. A historical recounting of industrialization's development would be incomplete without discussing diasporic contributions, especially those of the African Diaspora. The inclusion of diaspora in the world's historical development has been described as having "come at a time when many agencies are promoting bottom-up contextual policy interventions[144] and where a failing global development project champions nation-state and local community ownership of development process."[145] The African Diaspora has retained a consistently influential presence in global history and culture.

"Unfinished Migrations: Reflections on the African Diaspora and the Making of the Modern World,"[146] by Tiffany Patterson and Robin Kelley, offers insights

---

[142] World Bank, *Migration, Remittances, and Development in Africa* (Washington, DC: World Bank, 2011); United Nations Development Programme (UNDP), *Human Development Report*: *Overcoming Barriers – Human Mobility and Development* (New York: IDP, 2009); and World Bank, *Global Economic Prospects*: *Economic Implications of Remittances and Migration* (Washington, DC: World Bank, 2006).

[143] S. Hickey, "The politics of protecting the poorest: Moving beyond the 'anti-politics machine'," *Political Geography* 28, 8 (2009): 473–483.

[144] D. Hilhorst, I. Christoplos, and G. Van Der Haar, "Reconstruction 'from below': A new magic bullet or shooting from the hip?" *Third World Quarterly* 31, 7 (2010): 1107–1124.

[145] Hickey, "The politics of protecting the poorest," 481.

[146] Patterson and Kelley, "Unfinished migrations," 11–45.

into the African Diaspora's contributions to the "mapping of the modern world." They begin their argument by referencing the African Diaspora's contributions to the evolution and development of the "Atlantic." With examples from other African Diaspora scholars, including Brent Edwards and Cedric Robinson, Patterson and Kelley underscore the relevance of the Black Mediterranean in the Italian and Francophone worlds. They also recognize the importance and significance of the Black Indian Ocean, as identified by Joseph Harris and Edward Alpers.[147] Instead of barriers, the extensive bodies of water that facilitated the diasporic movements of Africans – especially during the fourth diasporic stream – served as multiple avenues for cultural transformation and exchange along with transoceanic and transnational trades.[148] The crossing of the Indian Ocean, as one example, created a mixture of people from India, East Africa, and the Arab world.[149]

Patterson and Kelley explain that the African Diaspora created a transformational framework that is also reflected in the studies of Marcus Rediker[150] and Peter Linebaugh.[151] In "The Many Headed Hydra: Sailors, Slaves, and the Atlantic Working Class in the Eighteenth Century,"[152] Rediker and Linebaugh underscore how the emergence of the transatlantic trade of African slaves and the merchant capital, complemented by shifting maritime power dynamics, created a new working class. These forces introduced a considerable amount of pauperization, but they were also the genesis of important political movements that included Pan-Africanism, Republicanism, and the more recent idea of internationalism.[153]

A similar approach can be seen in "The Common Wind: Currents of Afro-American Communications in the Era of the Haitian Revolution," by Julius

---

[147] Brent Edwards, "Black globality: The international shape of Black intellectual culture," Ph.D. diss., Columbia University, 1997; Cedric Robinson, *Black Marxism: The Making of the Black Radical Traditions* (London: Zed Press, 1983); Joseph Harris, *The African Presence in Asia: Consequences of the East African Slave Trade* (Evanston, IL: Northwestern University Press, 1971); and Edward Alpers, "The African Diaspora in the Northwestern Global Dimensions of the African Indian Ocean: Reconsideration of an old problem, new directions for Research," Paper presented at conference, "The Northwestern Global Dimensions of the African Indian Ocean as cultural corridor," Stockholm University, January 1997: 17–19.

[148] Joseph Harris, "A comparative approach to the study of the African Diaspora," in Jospeh Harris, (ed.), *Global Dimensions of the African Diaspora* 2nd ed., (Washington, D.C.: Howard University Press, 1982),112–124.

[149] K. N. Chaudhuri, *Asia before Europe: Economy and Civilization of the Indian Ocean from the Rise of Islam to 1750* (New York: Cambridge University Press, 1990).

[150] Marcus Rediker, *"Between the Devil and the Deep Blue Sea": Merchant Seamen, Privates, and the Anglo-American Maritime World, 1700–1750* (Cambridge: Cambridge University Press, 1987).

[151] Peter Linebaugh, "All the Atlantic mountains shook," *Labour/Le Travailleur* 10 (1982): 87–121.

[152] Peter Linebaugh and Marcus Rediker, "The many headed hydra: Sailors, slaves, and the Atlantic working class in the Eighteenth Century," *Journal of Historical Sociology* 3, (1990): 225–252.

[153] Linebaugh and Rediker, "The many headed hydra."

Scott.[154] Scott's work studies modern African people during the Haitian revolution, unveiling the metaphoric and literal meaning of what he describes as a "sailing image" that defines how networks of shared experiences and oral transmissions shaped the scope of diasporic identity and politics within the continent of Africa and beyond. Scott uses the Black population who originated from Africa to explain the emergence of a collective desire for antislavery republicanism. This development was more radical than contemporary ideas obtainable in France and Philadelphia, primarily due to the fact that it was politically driven. As a result, the new world was riven by various international organizations and ideological debates among African Americans. Patterson and Kelley state that Scott's demonstration of the Afro-diasporic approach, along with its roles and impacts, are evidence of the African Diaspora's contribution to "the creation of New World republicanism, systems of communication in the eighteenth and early nineteenth century, the political and cultural autonomy of African people in the West, and the crucial role that black sailors played in the age of democratic revolutions."[155]

Patterson and Kelley assert that the African Diaspora has greatly influenced and shaped every conceivable aspect of the modern West. This impact can be identified through a critical examination of post-emancipation communities. Their claims are similar to what other contemporary scholars, such as Frederick Cooper,[156] Thomas Holt,[157] David Eltis,[158] Rebecca Scott,[159] Robin Blackburn,[160] Eugene Genovese[161] – and their earlier twentieth-century predecessors, such as C. L.R. James[162] and W.E.B. Du Bois[163] – have demonstrated in their various scholarly

---

[154] Julius Scott, "The common wind: Currents of Afro-American communications in the era of the Haitian Revolution," Ph.D. diss, Duke University, 1986.

[155] Patterson and Kelley, "Unfinished migrations."

[156] Frederick Cooper, *From Slaves to Squatters: Plantation Labor and Agriculture in Zanzibar and Coastal Kenya 1890–1925* (New Haven: Yale University Press, 1980); and Frederick Cooper, Thomas Cleveland Holt, Rebecca J. Scott *Beyond Slavery: Explorations of Race, Labor, and Citizenship in Post-Emancipation Societies* (Chapel Hill: University of North Carolina Press, 2000).

[157] Thomas Holt, *The Problem of Freedom: Race, Labor and Politics in Jamaica and Britain 1832–1938* (Baltimore: Johns Hopkins University Press, 1992).

[158] David Eltis, "Europeans and the rise and fall of African slavery in the Americas: An interpretation," *American Historical Review* 98, 5 (1993): 1399–1423.

[159] Rebecca Scott, "Defining the boundaries of freedom in the World of Cane: Cuba, Brazil and Louisiana after emancipation," *American Historical Review* 99 (1990): 70–102.

[160] Robin Blackburn, *The Overthrow of Colonial Slavery 1776–1848* (London: Verso, 1988).

[161] Eugene Genovese, *The World the Slave Holders Made: Two Essays of Interpretation* (New York: Pantheon Books, 1970); and Eugene Genovese, *From Rebellion to Revolution: Afro-American Slave Revolts in the Making of the Modern World* (Baton Rouge: Louisiana State University Press, 1974).

[162] C. L. R. James, *The Black Jacobins: Toussaint L'Ouverture and the San Domingo Revolution* 2nd ed. (New York: Vintage Books, 1938).

[163] W. E. B. Du Bois, *Black Reconstruction in America 1860–1880* (New York: Atheneum Press, [1935] 1969); and W. E. B. Du Bois, *The World and Africa: An Inquiry into the Part Which Africa Played in World History* (New York: Viking, 1947).

contributions, especially regarding the transition from servitude and slavery to autonomy. The African Diaspora has been useful not only in global processes but also in the restoration of the labor force. It has left an enduring impression on global capitalism, racial ideology, and democracy.

Although Patterson and Kelley have mapped out the African Diaspora's significance through various scholarly sources, the majority of citations in "Unfinished Migrations," only relate to the Americas and Europe. Their work fails to analyze the African Diaspora's role in shaping cultural practices and historical evolutions elsewhere in the world, such as India, Asia, and the Middle East. Although their work illustrates Afro-diasporic roles played by persons of African descent on the continent itself, it is done scantily and without much focus. Their work is also limited by its exclusive focus on contributions made primarily by Western scholars. It could also have considered the African Diaspora's influence on religious developments, given that religion is a major aspect of African culture.

Conclusion

The current age of technological advancements and transformations makes it important to examine studies that focus on the continent of Africa in general and people of African descent in particular. The field of African Diaspora studies has garnered a substantial number of contributions from various scholars around the world,[164] but research and studies working to unravel the depth surrounding the phenomenon of the African Diaspora remain prevalent. An increasing body of research and studies has illustrated the need to rethink the African Diaspora. This can be facilitated by a critical review of major literature, books, and journals covering related subjects, including the traditional narrative of the African Diaspora, alternative perspectives on the African Diaspora, and the African Diaspora's role in shaping global history and culture. Contributions from scholars like Colin Palmer, Blaine Hudson, St. Clair Drake, Tiffany Patterson, Robin Kelley, and others have been immensely useful for this effort. As emerging African historians and scholars increase their understanding of previous scholarship and research, they can improve such studies in the future.

5 The Emergence of a New Global African Diaspora

Introduction

A reevaluation of the African Diaspora, from its inception to its current evolution, has been triggered by an increasing number of diasporic studies,

---

[164] Shepperson, "African Diaspora," 44.

continuous diasporic phenomena, scientific and technological innovations, recent enthusiasm for unraveling the complexities surrounding the Atlantic Diaspora, the emergence of global culture and capital, and the collapse of global communication boundaries and barriers. The nature and general composition of the African Diaspora have undergone a variety of transformations, from the involuntary movement of Africans and their descendants as slaves in the Old and New Worlds to the voluntary migration of skilled and free Africans in search of greener pastures – although this has also been described as "involuntary," due to the exploitative dynamics at work.

Africans are constantly in motion,[165] and although the African Diaspora had previously made little or no contact with its homeland, it has evolved into a social phenomenon that maintains active contact with various communities and societies across Africa. People of African descent exist in every culture and continent in the world, and every nontraditional place of migration has become home to people of African descent. These destinations include Australia, New Zealand, Taiwan, Japan, and Israel.

The diasporic movements of people have generated various sociological issues, including state–civil community relations, the conceptual clarification of citizenship, and the limitations of religion and culture. These concepts have been altered and debated as new developments arise from the proliferation of commercial diasporas within and beyond the continent. New questions have also been raised by the ongoing yet unexpected existence of involuntary labor in Africa and elsewhere.

The concept of an African Diaspora is complex and continually evolving and changing, which makes it challenging to define. However, the emphasis on the new global African Diaspora has recognized different spheres for African cultures and religions, financial capital applied toward continental development, economic and commercial benefits from the exodus of skilled African descendants, and the distinction of separate political milieus. Through these categorizations, the concept of African Diaspora becomes relatively relatable.[166]

Joseph Harris explains that there are myriad ways in which diasporas "affect the economies, politics, and social dynamics of both the homeland and the host country or area."[167] A definition of the African Diaspora should begin with a conceptual clarification of the latter word – a diaspora refers to a group of

---

[165] L. J. Legwaila, *The Role of the Diaspora in Support of Africa's Development* (London: African Leadership Diaspora Forum, 2006).

[166] Y. Kuznetsov, *Diaspora Networks and the International Migration of Skills: How Countries Can Draw on Their Talent Abroad* (Washington, DC: World Bank, 2006).

[167] Joseph E. Harris, "The dynamics of the global African Diaspora," in Alusine Jalloh, and Stephen E. Maizlish, (eds.), *The African Diaspora* (Arlington: Texas A & M University Press, 1996), 7.

persons who have moved or migrated from a specific area or country, commonly referred to as the homeland, to occupy another area or country, commonly called the host land, while they maintain bonds and connections with their homeland. Additional characteristics define diaspora as a phenomenon that involves more than mere migration.

The US State Department asserts that a diaspora has the following characteristics:

> dispersion, whether voluntary or involuntary, across sociocultural boundaries and at least one political border; a collective memory and myth about the homeland; a commitment to keeping the homeland alive through symbolic and direct action; the presence of the issue of return, though not necessarily a commitment to do so; as well as a diasporic consciousness and associated identity expressed in diaspora community media, creation of diaspora associations or organizations, and online participation.[168]

William Safran, one of the major scholars in the field of African Diaspora Studies, defines six specific criteria for the term:

> (1) they, or their ancestors, have been dispersed from a specific original "centre" to two or more "peripheral," or foreign, regions; (2) they retain a collective memory, vision, or myth about their original homeland-its physical location, history, and achievements; (3) they believe they are not and perhaps cannot be fully accepted by their host society and therefore feel partly alienated and insulated from it; (4) they regard their ancestral homeland as their true, ideal home and as the place to which they or their descendants would (or should) eventually return when conditions are appropriate; (5) they believe that they should, collectively, be committed to the maintenance or restoration of their original homeland and its safety and prosperity; and (6) they continue to relate, personally or vicariously, to that homeland in one way or another, and their ethno-communal consciousness and solidarity are importantly defined by the existence of such a relationship.[169]

According to the African Union, the term "African Diaspora" refers to "people of African origin living outside the continent, irrespective of their citizenship and nationality and who are willing to contribute to the development of the continent and the building of the African Union."[170] Several attempts have been made to estimate the size of the African Diaspora, but they fall short due to the complexity of the diaspora itself, which is further complicated by factors that

---

[168] US Department of State, Telegraph 86401, Washington DC, "Engaging with Diaspora Communities: Focus on EAP, EUR, and NEA," Summary Report, Foreign Service Institute Leadership and Management School Policy Leadership Division and the Global Partnership Initiative, Foreign Policy Institute, Office of the Secretary of State, Washington DC, 2010.

[169] William Safran, "Diasporas in modern societies: Myths of homeland and return," *Diaspora* 1, 1 (1991): 83–99.

[170] African Union (AU), *Report of the Meeting of Experts from Member States on the Definition of the African Diaspora* (Addis Ababa, April 11–12), 2005.

include questions of identity, periods and times of migration, citizenship, and place of birth.[171]

The size of US-based diasporas is often estimated with US census statistics, paying attention to the "place of birth for the foreign-born population." In other attempts to estimate the size of diaspora, in countries such as Japan, the Republic of Korea, and those belonging to the European Organization for Economic Co-operation and Development (OECD), immigrants are classified by their parental ethnicity; these results provide relatively larger numbers than estimates that rely on individual places of birth.[172] A diaspora can include large numbers of temporary immigrants that are often neglected in immigration data. Ultimately, the definition of a diaspora and the estimation of its size can be set by each country. In this light, India defines its diaspora as "people of Indian origin, non-resident Indian, and overseas citizenship of India."[173] The *Migration and Remittance Factbook 2011* calculated the size of the African Diaspora, counted as international emigrants of African descent, at 30.6 million as of 2010.[174]

The emergence of a new global African Diaspora has ushered in reasons to revisit the evolution of the African Diaspora and analyze its emergence while considering its impacts and contributions to the continent of Africa. There is a pressing need to review and examine research works, books, and literature that relate to the subject, along with other complementary concepts.

Revisiting the African Diaspora's Evolution

Africa's history of relations and interactions with the world is as old as humanity. An Afro-Atlantic account of the African Diaspora is inadequate on its own because the dispersal of African descendants is a story that is as old as history itself. Many research works, books, and journals cover the historical evolution of the African Diaspora, and despite the diaspora's many dimensions – ranging from diasporic movements across Europe to the trans-Saharan slave trade in the Muslim world and migrations to Asia – a majority emphasis has been placed on the Atlantic model that concerns the migration of Africans to the Americas.

---

[171] Rachel Murphy, "Migration and inter-household inequality: Observations from Wanzai County, Jiangxi," *The China Quarterly* 164 (2000): 965–982.

[172] Organization of Economic Co-operation and Development (OECD), *The Global Competition for Talent: Mobility of the Highly Skilled*, (Paris: OCED [Policy Brief], 2011); and, Organization of Economic Co-operation and Development (OECD), *The Contribution of Diaspora Return to Post-Conflict and Fragile Countries: Key Findings and Recommendations* (Paris: Partnership for Democratic Governance, Organization of Economic Co-operation and Development, 2010).

[173] Dina Ionescu, *Engaging Diaspora as Development Partners for Home and Destination Countries: Challenges for Policymakers* (IOM *Migration Research Series* No. 26) (Geneva: International Organization for Migration, 2006).

[174] World Bank, *Migration and Remittance Factbook 2011* (Washington, DC: World Bank, 2011).

Paul Zeleza's "African Diaspora: Towards a Global History" is a reliable source of reference for the African Diaspora's evolution. Zeleza begins his explanation of the African Diaspora's historical mappings by emphasizing that interest in the field of African Diaspora studies, particularly relating to Asia and Europe, is a new phenomenon. He undertakes a step-by-step approach to explain the evolution of the African Diaspora, acknowledging the challenges of tracing the origins of African descendants who have settled in Europe.

Zeleza argues that there are major differences regarding the formation, size, and periodization of African Diasporic movements across Europe. These movements were present in the Southern Europe of antiquity, dating back to the Roman era; Western Europe, dating back to the African conquest of the Iberian Peninsula; and Eastern and Central Europe, dating back to the medieval periods when a massive number of African soldiers were deployed in the Turkish armies during the Crusades and the expansion of the Ottoman Empire.[175] During these periods, European society was highly assimilative, and most of the individuals who survived their migrations ended up assimilating with local communities, as did their descendants. Some groups retained their own identities through separation, such as Abraham Hannibal's descendants,[176] while others retained memories of iconographic illustrations, archaeological artifacts, and more recent DNA studies.

Unlike the Afro-American diasporic movements, most of the African Diaspora in European nations consist of descendants or members of communities that have metamorphosed into the new diaspora. Zeleza expects the trends of the past to continue, which means that the trans-Atlantic component of the African Diaspora will continue to dominate the Americas. His example is "Afro-Latin America, where the extent of postcolonial African migration pales in comparison to the situation in Afro-North America."[177]

Zeleza finds a marked difference between the phenomena of intersecting diasporas in Europe and those in the Americas. This affects how identities are formed in the new diasporas and their patterns of integration, which introduces various degrees of class composition caused by the "social cost of relocation." Recent works on the Ghanaian diaspora in Europe and the United States, pioneered by John Arthur, attest to this fact.[178]

---

[175] Hine, Keaton, and Small (eds.), *Black Europe and the African Diaspora*.

[176] Issatas Tesfamariam, "Abraham P. Hannibal (Eritrea/Russia)," in Mary Esther Kropp Dakubu and Eva Maria Asante, (eds.), *African Visionaries* (Legon-Accra: Sub-Saharan Publishers, 2019), 164.

[177] Paul Tiyambe Zeleza, "The Changing Meanings of 'African' Culture and Identity," in Elisabeth Abiri and Hakan Thorn, (eds.), *Horizons: Perspectives on a Global Africa* (Göteborg, Sweden: National Museum of World Cultures and Göteborg University, 2006), 31–72.

[178] John A. Arthur, *The African Diaspora in the United States and Europe: The Ghanaian Experience* (Burlington, VT: Ashgate, 2008).

Zeleza notes that France, which is home to the largest contingent of the African Diaspora, houses no fewer than four categories of diasporas, including Antillean Blacks, pre-existing communities of African origin, Africans of North African descent, and Africans from Central and West African descent. In addition to the complexity with which these communities relate to each other, they also have complex associations with French societies and states. These relations create avenues for solidarities that can dictate and influence their existence based on place of descent, religion, race, country of birth, gender, and class. Many people of West African origin find themselves religiously associated with their North African counterparts, sub-regionally to their Central African counterparts, and racially to the Antilleans.[179]

After discussing the African Diaspora's evolution in Europe, Zeleza uncovers African Diasporic activities in Asia and its surrounding settlements. Before delving into Afro-Asian interactions and diasporic movements, he states that the Asian accounts are the most complicated of all the African diasporic histories. In "African Diasporas: Towards a Global History," Zeleza groups the African diasporic movements in Asia – specifically, the ones that followed the prehistoric era – into five periods. The first such period, identified as the ancient interactions, is subdivided into two aspects: Western Asia and Pharaonic Egypt interactions and connections between the Arabian Peninsula and ancient Ethiopia. Their major defining features were constant conquests and counter-conquests. Other interactions include the classical period, which evolved significantly during the Roman and Greek empires, the fifteenth- and sixteenth-century associations of the European period, the Islamic era interactions, and recent interactions that occurred after decolonization.

Zeleza explains that the rationale behind this periodization is primarily because global diasporic formations and demographic migrations are historically connected to the establishment, extension, breach, and realignment of empires. These interactions were enabled by the Mediterranean–Red Sea passage that connects Western Asia to Northern Africa, the Red Sea–Indian Ocean passage that connects Southern and Western Asia to North-Eastern Africa, and the Indian Ocean passage that connects Asia and the Indian Ocean islands to Eastern Africa.[180]

Over the past 2,000 years, sub-Saharan African migrations have followed three distinct patterns: "(1) to western Asia from the first millennia encompassing the regions between Arabia and Iran (2) to east and south Asia from

---

[179] Claire Alexander, "Beyond Black: Re-thinking the colour/culture divide," *Ethnic and Racial Studies* 25, 4 (2002): 552–571.

[180] Paul Tiyambe Zeleza, "Diaspora dialogues: Engagements between Africa and its diasporas," in Isidore Okpewho and Nkiru Nzegwu, (eds.), *The New African Diaspora* (Bloomington: Indiana University Press, 2009), 31–58.

the second millennia (3) to the Indian Ocean islands from the 15th century."[181] These migrations encouraged the free movement of people, including African soldiers, proselytes, merchants, and sailors who settled in the present-day continent of Asia. Involuntary movements of Africans and their descendants also occurred during this era, especially through European and Arab trade in African slaves.[182]

Prior to the twentieth century, the Indian Ocean enabled a substantial degree of African mobility. A significant quantity of literature covers the modalities of these movements, but Zeleza mentions that scholarly consensus had agreed that the demand for African labor was minimal in the desert regions of the Gulf and the densely populated Asian continent. After an intense examination and analysis of texts, this consensus shifted. Zeleza explains that the contributions of Shihan Jayasuriya and Richard Pankhurst in *The African Diaspora in the Indian Ocean*,[183] Jayasuriya in "African Cultural Identity in Asia: Cultural Effects of Forced Migrations,"[184] and Jayasuriya and Jean-Pierre Angenot in *Uncovering the History of Africans in Asia*[185] further explain this phenomenon.

The scope and period of Zeleza's work are constrained to the major diasporic movements of Africans in Europe and Asia. Although he mentions the transatlantic diaspora in the Americas, he does not explore its dynamics to the same degree as those of the African Diaspora in Europe and Asia. The history of the African Diaspora also extends beyond that of the New World – Colin Palmer's "Defining and Studying the Modern African Diaspora"[186] describes the premodern diasporic streams or ancestral diasporic movements that evolved into the New World Diaspora. Zeleza also raises questions regarding the nature of the sources and the penetrating influences of the Afro-Atlantic Diasporas that are left unanswered. He concludes by stating that "only more research will tell."

Mirroring the Emergence of a New Global African Diaspora

The contributions of scholars and historians have mirrored the emergence of a new global African Diaspora. Joseph Harris is one such scholar – his book, *Global Dimensions of the African Diaspora,* is an evergreen piece because of its

---

[181] Paul T. Zeleza, "African Diasporas: Toward a global history," *African Studies Review*, 53, 1 (2010): 12.

[182] Meghan Keita, "Africans and Asians: Historiography and the long-view of global interactions," *Journal of World History* 16, 1 (2005): 1–30.

[183] Jayasuriya and Pankhurst (eds.), *The African Diaspora in the Indian Ocean*.

[184] Shihan de Silva Jayasuriya, "African identity in Asia: Cultural effects of forced migration," *African Diaspora Archaeology Newsletter* 12, 3 (2009): 14.

[185] Shihan de Silva Jayasuriya and Jean-Pierre Angenot, (eds.), *Uncovering the History of Africans in Asia* (Leiden: Brill, 2008).

[186] Palmer, "Defining and studying the modern African Diaspora," 27–32.

revealing, all-inclusive identity. The African Diaspora has been described as having different phases that vary in space and time. In this light, Harris identifies four phases of the African Diaspora: the primary, secondary, tertiary, and circulatory phases. Harris writes that "the primary stage is the original dispersion out of Africa [especially through the slave trade]; the secondary stage occurs with migrations from the initial settlement abroad to a second area abroad; the tertiary stage is movement to a third area abroad; and the circulatory stage involves movements among the several areas abroad and may include Africa."[187]

Subsequent attempts have been made to unravel the mysteries surrounding the new global African Diaspora. Emmanuel Akyeampong's "Africans in the Diaspora: The Diaspora and Africa"[188] has been immensely useful in this regard, dividing the new global African Diaspora into three phases: the pre nineteenth, nineteenth, and twentieth-century African dispersions. Through these categorizations, Akyeampong examines the various channels and trajectories of dispersal for people of African origin. This examination begins with the African Diaspora's inception to more recent global migrations of Africans and the dispersion of their communities, which has greatly affected the direction of movement in Harris' circulatory phase, particularly in the twentieth century.

To emphasize the differences in diasporic experiences among Africans, Akyeampong attempts an unbiased extraction of the experiences and identities of Africans and their descendants during the pre nineteenth-century diasporic movements. Akyeampong stresses that free Africans were at liberty to travel within the Old and New Worlds even when the international slave trade was at its peak. The emancipation and abolition of slavery, which is the nineteenth century's characterizing feature in the general history of diaspora and diasporic streams, facilitated further migration and a diaspora influenced by frequent travel. This ultimately made the African Diaspora's dimensions more complex.[189]

Akyeampong's analysis begins with the pre nineteenth-century African Diaspora and reflects the three diasporic streams of trade in African slaves, which Patrick Manning emphasizes in his popular work *Slavery and African Life*. These streams include the internal trade in African slaves, the transatlantic slave trade, and the Asian or Muslim slave trade. These streams dispersed Africans to different parts of the world, including the Americas, Asia, Europe, and the Middle East.

---

[187] Joseph Harris, "Introduction", in Joseph Harris, (ed.), *Global Dimensions of the African Diaspora* (Washington, D.C.: Howard University, 1982), 8–9.

[188] Emmanuel Akyeampong, "Africans in the diaspora: The diaspora and Africa," *African Affairs* 99, 395 (2000): 183–215.

[189] James Clifford, "Diasporas," *Cultural Anthropology* 9, 3 (1994): 305–306; and Clifford, *Routes*.

Akyeampong asserts that obvious Black constituencies are responsible for much of the scholarly attention received by the African Diaspora in the New World, also described as a new global African Diaspora that encompasses South, North, and Central America, along with the Caribbean. From the sixteenth to the nineteenth centuries, approximately thirteen million people of African descent were forcefully sent to the Americas.[190] Slaves captured during this era worked in mines and on plantations.[191] The involuntary migration of Africans spurred the development of new economic and commercial systems in the Atlantic and the Mediterranean, far from the shores of Western Africa, which resulted in the emergence of plantation complexes. These new economic systems were initially financed by Italian capital, and the search for tropical lands to support these systems was facilitated by the Spanish and Portuguese. The plantation complex, which was fundamentally based on slave labor engaged in sugar farming, supported the continuous Western demand for slaves from Africa. This continued until the early 1900s, when slavery was abolished.[192]

Africans and their descendants have lived in Europe since the Middle Ages. This assertion is supported by Irish records of Vikings who captured Africans in North Africa as far back as 862 AD. These African captives were referred to as "blue men" in Dublin.[193] This marked the beginning of the African presence in Europe, and Black communities surfaced in Yorkshire, Bedfordshire, Manchester, Hull, Liverpool, London, and other British regions during the eighteenth century.[194] African communities, either enslaved or free, were also established in major European population centers, including Barcelona, Valencia, Cadiz, Rome, Venice, Paris, Marseilles, Lyon, Nantes, Orleans, and

---

[190] Curtin, *The Atlantic Slave Trade*. The exact figure given by Curtin is 9.566 million people; Joseph Inikori, (ed.), *Forced Migration: The Impact of the Export Slave Trade on African Societies*, (London: Hutchinson, 1981) revises Curtin's estimates and argues for a higher figure of 15.4 million. Harris endorses Inikori's figures; See Harris, "Dynamics of the global African Diaspora," 11.

[191] David Northrup, *The Atlantic Slave Trade* (Lexington: D. C. Heath, 1994); Klein, *African Slavery in Latin America and the Caribbean*; Stuart B. Schwartz, *Slaves, Peasants, and Rebels: Reconsidering Brazilian Slavery* (Urbana, IL: University of Illinois Press, 1992); Richard S. Dunn, *Sugar and Slaves: The Rise of the Planter Class in English West Indies, 1624–1713* (New York: W. W. Norton, 1972); Robert William Fogel, *Without Consent or Contract: The Rise and Fall of American Slavery* (New York: Norton, 1989); and David Eltis, *The Rise of African Slavery in the Americas* (Cambridge: Cambridge University Press, 2000).

[192] Philip D. Curtin, *The Rise and Fall of the Plantation Complex* (Cambridge: Cambridge University Press, 1990); and Sidney W. Mintz, *Sweetness and Power: The Place of Sugar in Modern History* (New York: Penguin Books, 1985).

[193] Folarin Shyllon, "Blacks in Britain: A historical and analytical overview," in Joseph Harris, (ed.), *Global Dimensions of the African Diaspora* 2nd ed. (Washington, D.C.: Howard University, 1982), 171.

[194] Shyllon, "Blacks in Britain," 172–177. See also Peter Fryer, *Staying Power*.

Lisbon from the fifteenth century.[195] Less research has been conducted on the presence of Africans in the Persian Gulf, Arabia, and Asia, but Akyeampong suggests that "African slaves in the Arab world were mostly eunuchs, slave-soldiers, and domestics, categories that did not facilitate their biological reproduction"; which explains the relative absence of distinct Black communities in the Middle East.[196]

Akyeampong supports his arguments with Ralph Austen's estimate of nine million African descendants who were carried north to the Muslim world during the trans-Saharan slave trade. This population of Africans consisted of 3 million people who were forced out between 1600 and 1900 and the preceding six million people who left between 600 and 1600. The existence of these Africans in Asian communities is reflected in the work of Joseph Harris and in a more recent publication by Edward Alpers.[197] These sources establish the continuous existence of ancient African communities in Arabia, Pakistan, India, Oman, Iraq, Iran, and Yemen.

Akyeampong states that the African Diaspora took a new dimension after the abolition of the slave trade in the nineteenth century. New settlements were established in West Africa, and people of African descent in the United States, Jamaica, and Britain were repatriated to their mother continent. Akyeampong describes the deportation of ex-slaves from Brazil to Nigeria, the Republic of Benin, Togo, and Ghana in the 1830s, and he notes that the nineteenth-century emancipation encouraged "Bombay Africans" to return to Kenya. Many victims of slavery had found their way back to Africa long before the nineteenth century – one such example is Ayuba Suleiman Diallo, also known as Job Ben Solomon, who made his return in the eighteenth century[198] – but the nineteenth century substantively reconnected Africans in the diaspora with their territories of origin. Akyeampong explains that this reconnection would become more evident over time in African travels within the continent and journeys between the continent and the New World.[199]

Akyeampong's "Africans in the Diaspora" explicitly maps the essential dimensions of the new global African Diaspora. However, it fails to identify contemporary issues that the African Diaspora face. One such issue, and arguably the most pressing, is brain drain. This has been described as a new

---

[195] Harris, "The dynamics of the global African Diaspora," 10.

[196] Akyeampong, "Africans in the diaspora," 8.

[197] Alpers, "The African Diaspora in the Northwest Indian Ocean," 61–80.

[198] Philip Curtin, "Ayuba Suleiman of Bondu," in Philip Curtin, (ed.), *Africa Remembered: Narratives by West Africans from the Era of the Slave Trade* (Madison: University of Wisconsin Press, 1967), 17–59.

[199] J. Lorand Matory, "The English of Brazil: On the diasporic roots of the Yoruba Nation," *Comparative Studies in Society and History* 41 (1999): 72–103.

phenomenon, but its omission from a description of the African Diaspora in the New World reflects a shortcoming in Akyeampong's work. Although he explains the culture and community of the African Diaspora, particularly for the period before 1800, he also fails to discuss the three African diasporic streams' economic and political nature. This may be due to the fact that most diasporic movements in the nineteenth century and afterward were more economic and commercial.

The Impact of the New Global African Diaspora on Africa

A wealth of studies and research have been conducted on the topic of diasporic migrations within and beyond the African continent. A sizable amount of these studies focus on the historical evolution of the African Diaspora, and others make contributions to the emergence, traditional narratives, and alternative perspectives of the subject. There are relatively fewer studies of the African Diaspora's impact on Africa despite the in-depth coverage of its role in global history and culture.

Despite this shortage, Sonia Plaza and Dilip Ratha's work, *Diaspora for Development in Africa*,[200] is a major reference. They list a number of ways in which diasporic movements can spur development in underdeveloped countries. The new global African Diaspora has tremendous potential for making a positive impact on the African continent, from monetary remittances – which they acknowledge as the most potent force for all-inclusive development – to research, investment, the promotion of trade, and the transfer of technology and knowledge. Plaza and Ratha note that the new global diaspora has taken a new turn; migrants now retain ties with their native countries and constantly contribute to their countries' development, which is a departure from the diasporic movements of the Old World that were characterized by voluntary and involuntary migration from the homeland, followed by settlement in host countries, integration into new environments, and the eventual abandonment of their countries of origin.[201]

Plaza and Ratha state that approximately thirty million Africans from sub-Saharan Africa and North Africa account for official records of international migrants, but the size of the African Diaspora is considerably larger after the inclusion of second- and third-generation migrants and unrecorded migrants.[202] As of 2010, Africa accrued a total of more than $US40 billion in migrant

---

[200] Sonia Plaza and Dilip Ratha, (eds.), *Diaspora for Development in Africa* (Washington, DC: World Bank Publications, 2011).

[201] Mohan and Zack-Williams, "Globalisation from below," 211–236.

[202] Oliver Bakewell, "In search of the diasporas within Africa/à la recherche des diasporas à l'intérieur de l'Afrique," *African Diaspora* 1, 1–2 (2008): 5–27.

remittances. Since that time, standards of living have improved greatly for Africans, especially among people with low incomes.

Beyond individual remittances, diasporic movements make other contributions to Africa's development. Plaza and Ratha describe collective remittances that promote the exchange of knowledge and philanthropic activities within the continent, improved access to international capital markets, and increased trade channels that have collectively facilitated the smooth exchange of goods and services internationally and within the continent. They note that statistically, the African Diaspora is capable of contributing US\$53 billion per year to Africa's development. However, these savings are invested externally instead of being mobilized for African development.[203]

Plaza and Ratha also state that African migrants within Africa have contributed more to continental development and growth than African Diasporas abroad. These contributions are often belittled and underestimated, but trade and trade links are highly productive in the diasporic world. Plaza and Ratha note that Diaspora Trade Councils have been founded as viable units to enhance smooth business networks and trade missions. Embassies from some African nations, such as Kenya and Ethiopia, operate in London and Washington, DC, to encourage trade and business forums that attract diaspora investors to their representative countries.[204] Similar trends are evident in direct investments; countries such as Nigeria, Rwanda, Kenya, and Ghana have productively engaged with their diasporas to improve and increase national investment.

Diaspora for Development in Africa explains how the new global African Diaspora has brought investment to Africa through personal remittances, collective remittances, trade, direct investment, and other activities. However, it fails to explore how the African Diaspora has affected Africa culturally, religiously, or politically. These are integral parts of diasporic studies, exploring how migrants and diasporas influence cultural and political activities, especially in their home countries. The work also excludes any discussion of negative impacts that the African Diaspora may have on the continent. The new global African Diaspora has brought benefits and challenges to Africa, and the omission of adverse effects restricts the scope of the book.

Conclusion

Although the dispersal of Africans across the world has many causes, its primary driver has been the increasing demand for labor from capitalists and

---

[203] Hein De Haas, "International migration, remittances and development: Myths and facts," *Third World Quarterly* 26, 8 (2005): 1269–1284.

[204] Organization of Economic Co-operation and Development (OECD), *The Contribution of Diaspora Return to Post-Conflict and Fragile Countries*.

the global political economy. The African Diaspora has witnessed significant changes in its nature and composition from its pre nineteenth-century origins. People of African descent had previously been extracted from their homelands by force, and now they are migrating voluntarily due to political and economic reasons. This is why the African Diaspora's evolution must be revisited to mirror the emergence of a new global African Diaspora. A major difference from the pre-modern diasporic streams is the fact that science and technology have enabled several ways for people in the African Diaspora to remain connected with their homelands, which encourages wealth flows from the diaspora to Africa. The new global African Diaspora has also triggered substantial developments in individual countries, including the establishment of domestic development projects that foster economic, political, social, and cultural improvements.

Conclusion

The African Diaspora's history is a rich and complicated tapestry of experiences, cultures, customs, and challenges. As one of history's most important and influential historical chronicles it has created the world we know today. This phenomenon has been defined by millions of individuals of African descent who have migrated around the globe. It has resulted in various communities that have contended with the impacts of slavery, racism, and colonialism.

In defining and exploring the African Diaspora, there has been an exchange of information speaking to the history and existence of the affected peoples. Although the intention has often been to inform and educate, some of these works not only failed to achieve these goals, but they also redirected the course of African knowledge about its history and its diaspora. There is a case for treating the existing body of work on the African Diaspora as a historiographic whole, which is why the present Element has been written.

The first topic, "What is the History of the African Diaspora?" is an essential starting point for any exploration of the concept. It presents a historical overview of African Diaspora populations, tracing their origins back to precolonial migrations and the transatlantic slave trade. It emphasizes the range of experiences within the African Diaspora, including different characteristics of forced and voluntary migrations that produced diasporic groups. This topic also considers how African Diaspora groups have battled for freedom and fought oppression, generating a rich history of cultural and political action.

The second topic, "Interrogating the Conception and Construction of African Diaspora History," emphasizes the need to critically examine prevalent narratives regarding the origins and experiences of the African Diaspora. These tales have been structured and distributed to disguise the range of experiences within the African Diaspora, which means that a critical viewpoint is necessary to comprehend how the historical construction of African Diaspora history has influenced our knowledge of this phenomenon.

The third topic, "African Dispersals and the Concept of Overlapping Diaspora," places the African Diaspora in a larger perspective – it must be seen in the light of global migrations and the idea of overlapping diaspora. It is important to acknowledge that African Diaspora populations are part of a larger global migratory history that has affected the course of global events. This issue delves into the range of experiences within the African Diaspora, emphasizing the importance of researchers in comprehending the complexity of this phenomenon.

"Rethinking the African Diaspora," the fourth topic, questions dominant narratives about the African Diaspora and emphasizes the need to recognize the agency and resilience of African Diaspora populations. It acknowledges the many ways in which African Diaspora populations have shaped world history and culture. The investigation of other viewpoints is critical for interacting with the African Diaspora's variety of experiences and opinions.

"The Emergence of a New Global African Diaspora," the fifth topic, assesses the African Diaspora's present situation. The growth of the African Diaspora and the formation of a new global African Diaspora must be acknowledged, and technological advancements and increasing global interconnectivity have pushed these developments. This topic focuses on the emerging global African Diaspora's influence on Africa, underlining the need to interact with the continent and its people in more equitable and meaningful ways.

Additional study and teaching on the African Diaspora will be required in the future. This will entail an investigation into the nuances of various diasporic experiences, questioning established narratives that have often concealed this diversity – the African Diaspora is not a unified whole. African Americans in the United States have endured markedly different experiences from Afro-Latinx people in Latin America or Afro-Caribbeans in the United Kingdom. It is necessary to acknowledge and investigate this diversity, challenging any simplified or homogenized view of the African Diaspora.

It is also necessary to question old myths that often minimize the diversity of the African Diaspora. Many traditional histories of the African Diaspora have been built around restricted and reductionist conceptions focused on the experiences of those who were enslaved. These can neglect the agency of individuals and their contributions to these communities. These assumptions must be questioned to promote a more nuanced, inclusive view of the African Diaspora. It is also essential to interact with the emerging global African

Diaspora and investigate how technology and globalization influence the lives and viewpoints of individuals of African heritage.

Better cultural interchange and understanding should be encouraged among various African Diaspora populations, as well as between these communities and their ancestral motherland. This can include cultural exchange programs, educational and research collaborations, and joint projects that enhance cultural awareness and mutual understanding. We must recognize and address the persistent effects of slavery, racism, and colonialism on African Diaspora populations, which involves raising consciousness and understanding of the historical and continuing repercussions of structural oppression. It will also involve participation in policy, education, and social action efforts to address these concerns.

The rise of a new global African Diaspora brings opportunities and challenges for populations in the African Diaspora and on the African continent. It can serve as a forum for more cooperation and a greater interchange of ideas and resources, which will result in greater economic and political empowerment for individuals of African origin. However, the worldwide African Diaspora continues to suffer from marginalization, systematic racism, and political and economic insecurity in many areas of the globe.

More study, education, and activism are required to properly comprehend the intricacies and repercussions of the African Diaspora's changing dynamics. Efforts should be made to promote and celebrate the variety and depth of African Diaspora cultures and experiences, and resources should be applied to solve the issues that African Diaspora groups face. By doing so, we can create a more egalitarian, inclusive society that honors and celebrates the accomplishments of Africans and their descendants.

Finally, the African Diaspora is a diverse phenomenon that resists simple classification or explanation. The many subjects covered in this Element highlight the importance of recognizing and engaging with the diverse range of experiences, viewpoints, and histories within the African Diaspora. It is critical to continue investigating and comprehending the African Diaspora, its roots, experiences, and current development.

Further Reading

Adi, Hakim. "The African Diaspora, 'Development' and Modern African Political Theory," *Review of African Political Economy*. 29, no. 92 (2002): 237–251.

Bauböck, Rainer, and Thomas Faist. *Diaspora and Transnationalism: Concepts, Theories and Methods*. Amsterdam: Amsterdam University Press, 2010.

Benesch, Klaus, and Geneviève Fabre, eds. *African Diasporas in the New and Old Worlds: Consciousness and Imagination*. Amsterdam: Rodopi, 2004.

Bernal, Victoria. "African Digital Diasporas: Technologies, Tactics, and Trends: Introduction," *African Diaspora*. 12, no. 1–2 (2020): 1–10.

Campt, Tina. "The Crowded Space of Diaspora: Intercultural Address and the Tensions of Diasporic Relation," *Radical History Review*. 83, no. 1 (2002): 94–113.

Chivallon, Christine. "Beyond Gilroy's Black Atlantic: The Experience of the African Diaspora," *Diaspora: A Journal of Transnational Studies*. 11, no. 3 (2002): 359–382.

Echeruo, Michael J. C. "An African Diaspora: The Ontological Project." In Isidore Okpewho, Carole Boyce Davies, and Ali Al'Amin Mazrui, eds., *The African Diaspora: African Origins and New World Identities*. Bloomington: Indiana University Press, 2001, 3–18.

Edwards, Brent Hayes. "The Uses of 'Diaspora'." In Klaus Benesch, and Geneviève Fabre, eds., *African Diasporas in the New and Old Worlds*. Amsterdam: Rodopi, 2004, 3–38.

Gordon, Edmund T., and Mark Anderson. "The African Diaspora: Toward an Ethnography of Diasporic Identification," *Journal of American Folklore*. 112, no. 445 (1999): 282–296.

Gunning, Sandra, Tera W. Hunter, and Michele Mitchell. "Gender, Sexuality, and African Diasporas," *Gender & History*. 15, no. 3 (2003): 397–408.

Hanchard, Michael. "Afro-Modernity: Temporality, Politics, and the African Diaspora," *Public Culture*. 11, no. 1 (1999): 245–268.

Koser, Khalid, ed. *New African Diasporas*, New York: Routledge, 2003.

Larson, Pier M. "African Diasporas and the Atlantic." In Jorge Canizares-Esguerra and Erik R. Seeman, eds., *The Atlantic in Global History*. New York: Routledge, 2017, 130–151.

Mercer, Claire, Ben Page, and Martin Evans, eds. *Development and the African Diaspora: Place and the Politics of Home*. London: Bloomsbury, 2009.

Mohan, Giles, and Alfred B. Zack-Williams. "Globalisation from Below: Conceptualising the Role of the African Diasporas in Africa's Development," *Review of African Political Economy.* 29, no. 92 (2002): 211–236.

Morehouse, Maggi. "African Diaspora theory: Here, There, and Everywhere," *Diasporas, Cultures of Mobilities. Race* 2 (2015): 19–32.

Okpewho, Isidore, and Nkiru Nzegwu, eds. *The New African Diaspora.* Bloomington: Indiana University Press, 2009.

Olaniyan, Tejumola, and James Hoke Sweet, eds. *The African Diaspora and the Disciplines.* Bloomington: Indiana University Press, 2010.

Orser Jr., Charles E. "The Archaeology of the African Diaspora," *Annual Review of Anthropology.* 27, no. 1 (1998): 63–82.

Scott, David. "That Event, This Memory: Notes on the Anthropology of African Diasporas in the New World," *Diaspora: A Journal of Transnational Studies.* 1, no. 3 (1991): 261–284.

Cambridge Elements ≡

Historical Theory and Practice

Printed in the United States
by Baker & Taylor Publisher Services